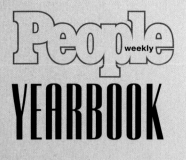

People weekly

YEARBOOK

The
Year in
Review
1998

STAFF FOR THIS BOOK

EDITOR: Eric Levin
SENIOR EDITOR: Richard Burgheim
ART DIRECTOR: Anthony Wing Kosner
SENIOR WRITER: Jill Smolowe
CHIEF OF REPORTERS: Denise Lynch
PICTURE EDITOR: Lila Garnett
DESIGNER: Scott G. Weiss
CONTRIBUTING WRITERS: Lynn Schnurnberger,
Nancy Stedman, Larry Sutton
COPY EDITOR: Dennison E. Demac
OPERATIONS: Jason Lancaster

Special thanks to Alan Anuskiewicz, Robert Britton, Betsy Castillo, Steven Cook, Orpha Davis, Tom Fitzgibbon, Brien Foy, David Geithner, Charles L. Guardino, George Hill, Suzy Im, Rachael Littman, Eric Mischel, Robert Mullins, James Oberman, Stan Olson, Stephen Pabarue, Jose Rua, Helen Russell, John Silva, Céline Wojtala, Desirée Yael Vester

Copyright ©1998 Time Inc. Home Entertainment
Published by

A division of Time Inc. Home Entertainment
1271 Avenue of the Americas
New York, NY 10020

PRESIDENT: David Gitow
DIRECTOR, CONTINUITIES AND SINGLE SALES: David Arfine
DIRECTOR, CONTINUITIES AND RETENTION: Michael Barrett
DIRECTOR, NEW PRODUCTS: Alicia Longobardo
GROUP PRODUCT MANAGERS: Robert Fox, Jennifer McLyman
PRODUCT MANAGERS: Christopher Berzolla, Roberta Harris, Stacy Hirschberg, Kenneth Maehlum, Daniel Melore
MANAGER, RETAIL AND NEW MARKETS: Thomas Mifsud
ASSOCIATE PRODUCT MANAGERS: Carlos Jimenez, Daria Raehse, Niki Viswanathan, Betty Su, Lauren Zaslansky, Cheryl Zukowski
ASSISTANT PRODUCT MANAGERS: Jennifer Dowell, Meredith Shelley
EDITORIAL OPERATIONS DIRECTOR: John Calvano
BOOK PRODUCTION MANAGER: Jessica McGrath
ASSISTANT BOOK PRODUCTION MANAGER: Joseph Napolitano
FULFILLMENT DIRECTOR: Michelle Gudema
ASSISTANT FULFILLMENT MANAGER: Richard Perez
FINANCIAL DIRECTOR: Tricia Griffin
FINANCIAL MANAGER: Amy Maselli
ASSISTANT FINANCIAL MANAGER: Steven Sandonato
MARKETING ASSISTANT: Ann Gillespie

Special thanks to Anna Yelenskaya

HARDCOVER ISBN:1-883013-57-7
ISSN:1522-5895

We welcome your comments and suggestions about PEOPLE Books. Please write to us at:

PEOPLE Books
Attention: Book Editors
PO Box 11016
Des Moines, IA 50336-1016

If you would like to order any of our Hard Cover Collector Edition books, please call us at 1-800-327-6388 (Monday through Friday, 7 a.m.— 8 p.m., or Saturday, 7 a.m.— 6 p.m. Central Time).

PRECEDING PAGE: GERI HALLIWELL (CHRIS BUCK/OUTLINE). THIS PAGE (TOP TO BOTTOM): CHRIS ROCK (CRAIG BLANKENHORN/OUTLINE); HARRISON FORD (MICHAEL O'NEILL). FOLLOWING PAGE (TOP TO BOTTOM): PAUL AND LINDA McCARTNEY (PHOTOFEST); TARA LIPINSKI (JIM MALUCCI/OUTLINE)

61 Afraid to coast at 33, **CHRIS ROCK** worries, "Here today, David Cassidy tomorrow."

14 The force remains with **HARRISON FORD,** crowned the sexiest guy on the globe at age 56.

PRECEDING PAGE: At 25, Ginger left the Spice rack and reverted to Geri Halliwell, trading her trashy topless past for a new, tony image.

2

CONTENTS

40 After 29 years of total togetherness, **PAUL McCARTNEY** lost his soulmate, **LINDA.**

76 Having conquered the world at 15, **TARA LIPINSKI** became a girl who just wanted to have fun.

PEOPLE'S PEOPLE
Honoring our annual pop pantheon of Intriguers, Beauties, Best & Worst Dressed, Sexiest Men . . . 4

HEADLINERS
Bill Clinton faced truth and consequences, Michael J. Fox shared a sad secret, a grappler became a governor, Farrah flipped, and more 16

PARTY ANIMALS
Award nights are the defining fashion events of our day, when celebs glitter and gush 46

SENSATIONS
Love that Leonardo! While Slammin' Sammy and Big Mac launched missiles, Spices spooned . . . 62

SECOND CHANCES
John Glenn orbited anew, Marv Albert aired and repaired, medals caught up with heroes 82

FAMILY MATTERS
Sharon Stone, Barbra Streisand, Kate Winslet wed, Bruce & Demi split, Jodie Foster delivered 88

TRIBUTE
We will always have the songs of Frank Sinatra and Tammy Wynette, the wisdom of Dr. Spock, the dances of Jerome Robbins 106

3

People's

PEOPLE

When our weekly flagship *lists*, it's not like the *Titanic*. Celebrate with us again the luminaries who captured our fancy and brightened our pages in 1998:

- THE 25 MOST INTRIGUING PEOPLE
- THE 50 MOST BEAUTIFUL PEOPLE
- THE BEST & WORST DRESSED
- THE SEXIEST MEN ALIVE

KATIE COURIC
Losing her husband, lawyer Jay Monahan, 42, to colon cancer in January taught the *Today* show coanchor a vital lesson. "Life is tenuous and short," Couric, 41, said a few months later. "Don't let the b.s. get in the way of what's really important." Her priorities are daughters Elinor, 6, and Caroline, 2. But a new NBC contract guarantees that Couric will also continue as one of TV's favorite morning stars.

The American People

Judy Blume, *60, author*

James Brolin, *58, actor*

Hillary Clinton, *51, First Lady*

Katie Couric, *41, TV anchor*

Cameron Diaz, *26, actress*

Leonardo DiCaprio, *24, actor*

Matt Drudge, *32,*
Internet gossip

Calista Flockhart, *34, actress*

Michael J. Fox, *37, actor*

Edward Fugger, *56,*
reproduction scientist

John Glenn, *77,*
senator, astronaut

Alan Greenspan, *72,*
Federal Reserve chairman

Geri Halliwell, *26,*
Spice Girl

Lauryn Hill, *23,*
singer/songwriter

David Kaczynski, *49,*
brother of the Unabomber

Joan Kroc, *60,*
philanthropist

Emeril Lagasse, *39, chef*

Camryn Manheim, *37, actress*

Mark McGwire, *35,*
baseball hero

Chris Rock, *33, actor/comic*

Adam Sandler, *32,*
actor/comic

Ken Starr, *51,*
independent counsel

Oprah Winfrey, *44,*
talk show host/actress

The World War II soldier

CHRIS ROCK

Two blockbuster films (*Lethal Weapon 4* and *Dr. Doolittle*), a bestselling novel and a hit CD made 1998 a very good year for HBO's quick-witted headliner. But he's not ready to rest on his royalties. "Never accept anything in this business," says Rock, 33. "Here today, David Cassidy tomorrow." He doesn't just coast on attitude, says Conan O'Brien. "He puts the work in."

NEVE CAMPBELL Her best features, says her *Wild Things* costar Kevin Bacon, are "really beautiful eyes and a nice spirit." They help project the youthful naïveté necessary to make believable both troubled Julia Salinger on television's *Party of Five* and nice girl Sidney Prescott in the *Scream* movies. "My face can seem very innocent on-camera," reckons Campbell.

PEOPLE'S 50 MOST BEAUTIFUL PEOPLE OF 1998

Erykah Badu, *27, singer*

Celine Balitran, *23, teacher's aide/model*

Anne Bancroft, *66, actress*

Halle Berry, *31, actress*

Tony Blair, *45, prime minister of Great Britain*

Andrea Bocelli, *39, singer*

Neve Campbell, *24, actress*

Chris Carter, *41, TV producer*

Ann Curry, *41, news anchor*

Sandy Dalal, *21, menswear designer*

Matt Damon, *27, actor*

Cameron Diaz, *25, actress*

Leonardo DiCaprio, *23, actor*

Calista Flockhart, *33, actress*

Brendan Fraser, *29, actor*

Troy Garity, *24, actor*

Sarah Michelle Gellar, *21, actress*

Anne Heche, *28, actress*

Helen Hunt, *34, actress*

Enrique Iglesias, *23, singer*

Angelina Jolie, *22, actress*

Malia Jones, *21, model/surfer*

Anna Kournikova, *16, tennis player*

Ilia Kulik, *20, figure skater*

Ali Landry, *24, model*

Bai Ling, *27, actress*

Julia Louis-Dreyfus, *37, actress*

Cindy Margolis, *29, queen of the Internet*

Julianna Margulies, *31, actress*

(continued on following page)

JAMES VAN DER BEEK The aw, shucks, attitude of this six-foot, *Dawson's Creek* star goes a long way toward explaining his boyish charm. "My agent told me that there were momentary flashes when I reminded him a tad of Jimmy Stewart," he says. "That was the nicest compliment."

MOST BEAUTIFUL

(continued)

Dylan McDermott, *36, actor*

Brian Stokes Mitchell, *39, actor*

Paolo Montalban, *24, actor*

Olivia Newton-John, *49, singer/actress*

Stevie Nicks, *50, singer*

Gwyneth Paltrow, *25, actress*

Bernard C. Parks, *54, L.A. police chief*

Alex Rodriquez, *22, shortstop, Seattle Mariners*

Arundhati Roy, *38, author*

Tom Selleck, *53, actor*

Danny Seo, *20, environmental activist*

Will Smith, *29, actor/rapper*

Gloria Stuart, *87, actress*

Rob Thomas, *26, singer*

Blaine Trump, *41, socialite*

Hunter Tylo, *35, actress*

James Van Der Beek, *21, actor*

Chris Waddell, *30, actor/athlete*

Brian White, *24, country singer*

Prince William, *16, Eton student*

Catherine Zeta Jones, *28, actress*

CAMERON DIAZ There's something about the way she smiles that sets one of Hollywood's hottest young actresses apart from the crowd. "She has an energy, an electricity in her face—a sparkle that is unmistakable," says photographer Jeff Dunas. Adds costumer Leesa Evans: "She doesn't get too caught up in overanalyzing what beauty is."

DYLAN McDERMOTT "The man is liquid sex," says Camryn Manheim, his costar on the law drama *The Practice*. A confident McDermott won't quibble. "It takes a long time to get comfortable with your looks," he says.

BEST-DRESSED

PEOPLE'S BEST-DRESSED CELEBS OF 1998 Tyra Banks, *24, model;* Brandy, *19, singer, actress;* Sandra Bullock, *34, actress;* Sean "Puffy" Combs, *28, rapper, music producer;* Harry Connick Jr., *31, singer;* Cameron Diaz, *26, actress;* Minnie Driver, *28, actress;* Greg Kinnear, *35, actor;* Princess Marie-Chantal of Greece, *29, wife of Crown Prince Pavlos;* Gwyneth Paltrow, *25, actress*

SEAN "PUFFY" COMBS embodies a vision of Versace.

GWYNETH PALTROW premieres a Donna Karan at the movies.

MINNIE DRIVER sizzles in a red-hot Halston at the Oscars.

BILLY BOB THORNTON won't dress. Don't ask him.

CARMEN ELECTRA short-circuits in this Marc Bouwer item.

EMMA THOMPSON is too cute for comfort in an Issey Miyake.

WORST-DRESSED

PEOPLE'S WORST-DRESSED CELEBS OF 1998 Carmen Electra, *26, actress;* Kathy Griffin, *32, comedian;* Ethan Hawke, *27, actor;* Alex Kingston, *35, actress;* Debbie Matenopoulos, *23, TV cohost;* Lorrie Morgan, *39, singer;* Emma Thompson, *39, actress;* Billy Bob Thornton, *43, actor-writer-director;* Sigourney Weaver, *48, actress;* Peta Wilson, *27, actress*

SEXIEST MEN

PEOPLE'S SEXIEST MEN ALIVE, 1998 Harrison Ford, *56, actor* Mark McGrath, *30, rock star* Elvis Grbac, *28, athlete* Carson Daly, *25, broadcaster* Mark Vanderloo, *30, model* David Breashears, *42, explorer* Peter Phillips, *21, royal* Usher, *20, R&B star* John F. Kennedy Jr., *37, magazine editor* Kenneth Cole, *44, businessman* Gary Allan, *30, country star* Ingo Rademacher, *27, soap star* Steven Petersen, *37, animal lover*

HARRISON FORD
"Everybody is goo-goo-eyed over Harrison," says Melanie Griffith, his costar in 1988's *Working Girl.* "He's just so handsome and sweet and elegant and cool and macho."

USHER The R&B phenom keeps fit by doing up to 1,000 stomach crunches daily. And if that's not enough to attract the ladies, adds daytime actress Adrienne Frantz, "he's a great kisser."

While Lewinsky hid
from sight, this archive
photo from 1996 and its
much-run video version
became an inescapable
news image of 1998.

White House Sex, Lies and Videotape

Clinton's dalliance, then defiance, led stunningly to his impeachment

History may well remember the incident as an unimportant, if unseemly, scandal that damaged the legacy of a popular, two-term President (perhaps with a footnote explaining the meaning of "thong"). But as anyone living in the late 20th century knows, Bill Clinton, 52, experienced 1998 as the Year of *L'Affaire* Lewinsky. From the moment America—or at least its chattering elements—caught its first glimpse of the flirtatious, twentysomething White House intern in her perky beret, there was no escaping the sex scandal and its fallout of moral outrage, political squabbling, legal maneuvering and late-night TV punch lines.

The sordid melodrama started in January with President Clinton's six-hour deposition in the case of Paula Jones, the Arkansas woman who claimed she'd once been sexually harassed by then-Governor Clinton. After surviving the humiliation of being the first sitting President to be questioned as a defendant in a court case, Clinton thought the worst was over. It had, in fact, barely begun. Within days the name Monica Lewinsky entered the popular lexicon, along with charges a) that she and Clinton had frolicked in the Oval Office; b) that both had lied about the liaison while testifying under oath in the Jones case; c) that she had boasted about her sexploits to her friend Linda Tripp, who secretly recorded the girlish confidences, then turned them over to the Office of the Independent Counsel. This was the same IC—Kenneth Starr—who, after four years of rooting around in the Clintons' Whitewater land deal, Vincent Foster's death, Travelgate, Filegate and other possible improprieties, still had seemingly nothing to show. Now he sought and obtained what amounted to an open ticket to probe the President's Achilles heel: serial infidelity.

To make his case, Starr compelled mother (Monica's) to testify against daughter; attorney against client (President); Secret Service agents against the man they protect (code name: Potus). American parents were soon squirming as they tried to explain the inexplicable to their kids after the release of the six-volume Starr Report, with some 2,800 pages of often X-rated evidence. In addition, Clinton's videotaped testimony in the Lewinsky matter was broadcast in its entirety on TV, also courtesy of the 21 Republicans on the House Judiciary Committee.

In late fall, voters rendered their preliminary verdict on the mess by using the two weapons modern democracy affords: their vote and their TV remote. In a stunning Election Day upset, the Republicans, expecting to cash in on the tawdry case, actually lost five House seats. Speaker Newt Gingrich, 55, promptly resigned his leadership post and announced he would retire. As for the impeachment proceedings, the public signaled its disgust by not tuning into November's televised hearings with its original cast of one: Ken Starr. Even as Starr handled the posturing, pontificating and praise of 37 verbose representatives with aplomb, questions were circulating about his conduct. By then, Starr had quietly—and, many felt, belatedly—allowed that he'd found no impeachable offenses in any of his multiple areas of investigation, save Clinton's misstatements and obstructions to cover up his dalliance.

The White House counterattacked, charging Starr with leaking grand jury testimony and colluding with Linda Tripp to entrap the President. Partisan lines only hardened, and in a dramatic vote, Clinton was impeached on charges of perjury and obstruction of justice. Efforts began immediately to prevent a Senate trial of the President (the second in history and first since 1868) from paralyzing Washington. Meanwhile the rest of Americans got on with their lives, among them the women in Clinton's life. Paula Jones, 32,who had threatened an appeal after her case was thrown out of court, settled for $850,000. Monica Lewinsky, 25, who had maintained her silence throughout, signed a $600,000-plus-bonuses book deal, with text by Princess Diana biographer Andrew Morton. And Hillary Clinton, 51, who'd once taken a drubbing in the polls for insisting she wasn't "some little woman" standing by her man, saw her approval ratings soar—for standing by her own imperfect man.

The Righteous and Contentious Inquisitor

His friends describe Kenneth Starr as honest, evenhanded and scrupulously ethical. But as Independent Counsel, he came under attack for pursuing and expanding his investigation with partisan zealotry. A straight-arrow minister's son who eschews foul language, Starr, 51, also helped introduce the subject of oral sex to the national discourse.

The Kiss-and-Tell Friend Who Managed to Give Enemies a Good Name

In her high school yearbook, Linda Carotenuto listed as her pet peeve "a certain fair-weather friend." The young woman, who later married, divorced and became Linda Tripp, had apparently experienced early on the pain of disloyalty. Yet it was Tripp, now 49, who set a new standard for false friendship when she encouraged Lewinsky to share confidences about her relationship with the "big he," then secretly taped them, first on her phone machine, then by wearing a body wire. As reports surfaced that Tripp pressed Lewinsky to save a semen-stained blue dress, goaded the hapless intern into pestering Clinton for job outplacement and had been in touch with Starr's office since '94, her already low public popularity hit bottom.

The Accuser Whose Charges Started It All

As her legal showdown neared, Paula Jones got rid of the big-hair look (left), muted her makeup and donned more conservative attire (center). When her 15 minutes of fame expanded to 20, she got a nose bob as well (right).

"I did not have sexual relations with that woman, Ms. Lewinsky"

On January 26, as the first charges of Oval Office improprieties surfaced, an indignant Clinton, buttressed by a First Lady who seemed to believe him, wagged his finger at the American people and vehemently denied any wrongdoing.

The Still-Functioning First Family

After the televised August apology, the First Family headed for a 12-day vacation on Martha's Vineyard to celebrate Clinton's 52nd birthday and begin the difficult process of healing.

The Evolution of a Humiliating Apology

Hours after his grand jury appearance, Clinton went on TV, supposedly to apologize to the nation. But when the President came off as more defensive than remorseful, offering only a terse admission that his adulterous relationship had been "not appropriate," he set off fresh indignation. By mid-September (below, at a prayer breakfast) he contritely admitted, "I don't think there is a fancy way to say, 'I have sinned.'"

The President on the Hot Seat

Through four hours of testimony via videotape, before a grand jury on August 17, President Clinton explained and cajoled, pleaded, scolded and evaded. Mostly, though, he played to the camera, assuming that the tape would eventually find its way into the public domain. Sure enough, by September 21, the videotape was everywhere on network TV.

The Woman Who, Through It All, Stood by Her Philandering Man

The aftermath of marital infidelity is never a cakewalk. For the Clintons, the glare of public attention and embarrassment only added to the pressure. "The tragedy is that most of us endure such things as infidelity in secret. But the Clintons live in a fishbowl," says Jesse Jackson, who counseled the First Couple the night before the President publicly acknowledged his behavior. In the days after Clinton's tight-lipped confession, the prurient question foremost on people's minds was: What did Hillary know, and when did she know it? While no one knew precisely what went on behind the door of their holiday cottage, it was clear this was no ordinary vacation. There were no impromptu jogs on island bike paths, no sign of the presidential cart rambling over the golf links. At one party, a guest observed, "They weren't frosty, they weren't warm and cuddly, they were just kind of correct." Hillary's friends, who were convinced the Lewinsky affair had been a shocking blow to the First Lady, suggested she would be guided by the same resources she has relied on in the past: her religiously-based moral compass, a 23-year investment in the man she seemingly adores and, of course, her love for 18-year-old Chelsea.

A Convoluted Family Drama

Two girls got switched at birth, and the human tragedy had only begun

This is a 1998 story that encompasses many of the problems bedeviling our society—divorce, illegitimacy, highway death, bureaucratic breakdown. At first it also seemed to symbolize an admirably civilized response to such difficulties, but then it deteriorated into yet another distressing phenomenon of the times—runaway litigiousness. It all started shortly after an Independence Day auto accident in the Blue Ridge Mountains of Virginia that killed Kevin Chittum, 25, and

"It's been one terrible year," says Larry Chittum (with wife Rosa Lee). "If it wasn't for bad luck, we wouldn't have any luck at all." The photos on the mantelpiece depict some of the participants in their shared pain. Framed at top right are the Chittums' late son Kevin and his fiancée, Whitney Rogers, holding Rebecca and Lindsey, the children they were building a new house for and had raised until July 4th. That was the day Kevin and Whitney were killed in a car crash.

his fiancée, Whitney Rogers, 19. Their orphaned 3-year-old daughter, Rebecca, the grieving family soon discovered, was not biologically theirs; she had been switched at birth with another child in a Charlottesville hospital. Rebecca's birth mother was actually a woman named Paula Johnson, 31; and the little girl Johnson had been raising, Callie, was Chittum and Rogers's biological daughter. Rather than uproot the girls from the only relatives they had ever known, the families involved decided to leave things the way they were: Callie with Johnson, and Rebecca dividing her time among the people she called her grandparents—the parents of Chittum and Rogers. Though it happens two or three times a year in the U.S., there are no rules for how to proceed when a hospital mistakenly switches infants. And given the circumstances, this seemed to be a hopeful, almost Solomonic solution.

The families began by simply getting to know each other better. In early August, Johnson drove first to the Chittums', then to the Rogerses'. "There was a lot of crying and laughter and swapping of stories," recalled Johnson. Later that month the two girls met and played together for the first time. By summer's end all the parties had agreed to embrace the other child and her clan.

But, in November, the Rogerses had a change of heart and filed suit against the Chittums. They sought sole custody of Rebecca and the end of the earlier agreement between the sets of grandparents. All of them lived conveniently close in the Buena Vista, Virginia, area, and according to the original rotation arrangement, Rebecca (and Lindsey, a younger, second daughter also left behind by Kevin and Whitney) would spend four months a year with the Chittums; four more with Tom Rogers and his second wife, Brenda; and the other four with Tom's ex-wife Linda Rogers. Then the Chittums announced their intention to countersue for sole custody. And back across the state in Ruckersville, Paula Johnson took the Rogerses to task for callously breaking the fragile peace. "I thought everything we were doing was in the best interests of the kids," says Johnson. "And this is not in the best interests of the kids."

What caused the rift was the Rogerses' concern that Johnson was being encouraged to develop a relationship with Rebecca too rapidly. The Chittums had invited Johnson and Callie as overnight guests in their home, and when parents' night came at Rebecca's preschool, they brought Paula along. For her part, Johnson says she

Paula Johnson reared Callie (above at 2) and says she'd go to the Supreme Court to keep contact with birth daughter Rebecca.

was "surprised and hurt" by the Rogerses' custody petition, which she fears could keep her away from her biological child. Linda Rogers denies that, explaining, "I want Rebecca as the years go by to know Paula better, but this is going to be a slow, gradual process." Johnson, insisting that she had no desire to disrupt Rebecca's life, says, "I only want to take her to McDonald's, the playground, shopping, whatever moms and daughters do."

At that point people close to the case feared that the legal wrangling might spur Johnson to seek custody of Rebecca. But Johnson maintains she would never take Rebecca away from the people she has known as her grandparents. To do so, she realizes, would also mean separating Rebecca from Lindsey, the little girl she calls her sister; that, says Johnson, would be unconscionable.

Meanwhile, Johnson, a construction worker, was preparing to sue the University of Virginia Medical Center, where the baby switch occurred. Johnson, who is raising four children by three different fathers, had split with and never married Rebecca's father, Carlton Conley, 34. Indeed, it was court-ordered blood tests they underwent to prove paternity of Callie that led to the discovery of the maternity ward mix-up. A subsequent State of Virginia investigation failed to determine a culprit but concluded that there was no evidence of foul play. The one positive development is that over the past year, the Charlottesville medical center has tightened its security procedures to avoid a repetition.

And despite all the bickering among the grown-ups, the girls were reportedly doing well under the circumstances. Callie and Rebecca have been encouraged to call each other sister and have become close playmates despite their different temperaments. Rebecca is somewhat reserved while Callie is much more outgoing. Callie, in fact, has a sense that she is someone special. When she happens to see references to the case on television, says Johnson, she blurts out, "That's me! I'm the switched baby." Though Rebecca, like Callie, has been spared all the details, she remains understandably traumatized by the death of her original parents. "She asks about them every day," reports Linda Rogers. "You tell her, 'Mommy and Daddy are in heaven.' And she says, 'Who put them there?' And you say, 'God.'"

It was perhaps also the Lord who in mid-December brought a welcome truce between the feuding families. On the eve of a court trial, all the grandparents agreed to joint custody of Rebecca as well as liberal visitation rights for her biological mother.

And the Beat Goes On...

After Sonny Bono dies in a ski accident, his wife, Mary, secures his House seat

He was, it sometimes seemed, like one of those magically self-righting, punching-bag dolls. Knock him down and he would bounce back up irrepressibly, casting himself in roles that nobody would have imagined for him: Songwriter. Singer. TV star. Half of the superduo Sonny and Cher. Mayor. Congressman. Sonny Bono never tired of reinventing himself, and everything had come together for him. At 62, he was settled into both a cozy family life with wife Mary, 36, and their two children, Chesare, 9, and Chianna, 6, and a successful career on Capitol Hill. Because Bono had worked so hard for his happiness—he'd survived three failed marriages and multiple career setbacks—his death on a ski slope on

January 5th in South Lake Tahoe, California, seemed all the more tragic. He was skiing on an intermediate slope with his family when Chianna took a minor tumble. After Mary and Chesare stopped to help her, Bono told Mary he was going to go down in another direction. Heading off the groomed path and in among the trees, as skilled skiers often do, Bono apparently struck a 40-foot pine tree head-on and died instantly. (In November, Mary told *TV Guide* that prescription painkillers and tranquilizers Bono was taking had impaired his judgment. Yet the autopsy found no drugs in his body.)

At his public funeral, the roster of mourners aptly reflected Bono's varied life: House Speaker Newt Gingrich. Vice President Dan Quayle. Gay activist daughter

Chastity. Tony Orlando. Before 1,200 mourners, second wife Cher spoke affectionately of the man whose name will always be joined with hers. "Certain people thought that Sonny wasn't to be taken seriously because he allowed himself to be the butt of jokes," Cher said. "What people don't realize is that he created Sonny and Cher. . . . He had the confidence to be the butt of the joke because he created the joke."

The third child of Italian immigrant Santo, a truck driver, and Jean, a beautician, Salvatore Phillip Bono was a class clown who dropped out of high school and took a job as a butcher's delivery boy. But he had plans. Already writing songs, Bono wrangled a delivery route along Sunset Boulevard, where all the independent record labels were located. In the early '60s he landed a job at Phillies Records, where he edited tapes, noodled with sound engineering and sang background for the Ronettes and the Righteous Brothers. In 1964 the Searchers turned a tune he'd cowritten, "Pins and Needles," into a major hit. Then he met a 16-year-old runaway named Cherilyn Sarkisian La Piere, and everything changed. Sonny and Cher made it big in 1965, singing what would become their anthem, his "I Got You Babe." Two more Top 10 hits followed that year, along with his-and-hers nose jobs. But by the time that their CBS *Sonny and Cher Comedy Hour* debuted in 1971, they were on the skids. After Cher filed for divorce in 1974, her career crested as his sank.

Again Bono found his way back. He opened a restaurant, then met and married Mary. Eventually, he was elected mayor of Palm Springs, California, and in 1994 was swept into Congress in the GOP landslide. Three months after Bono's death, Mary gained his seat in a special election, then in November was reelected to a full term. Bono, who Mary says, "always made me feel like an equal partner," might find her victory a fitting coda.

Of Cher and Chas, Sonny wrote in his diary, "I would not trade those 10 years for anything."

Her moving, insightful eulogy, said Cher, "is the most important thing I've ever done."

After her two-to-one win over Ralph (*The Waltons*) Waite in April (below), Mary said, "I will do my best to live up to [Sonny's] legacy."

Mortal Lessons

Children with guns turn two public schools into killing grounds

Jonesboro mourned, on street signs (top) and at a local cemetery.

Martyred sixth-grade teacher Wright had posed with her son Zane on his first birthday.

Golden was "not a natural-born killer," said his granddad, who'd introduced him to guns early.

Shortly after lunch, as Shannon Wright's sixth-grade class was preparing to go to computer lab, the fire alarm sounded. "Someone had told me the principal was going to stage a play to show us what to do in case it was the real thing," recalls Emma Pittman, 12. "So we lined up and went outside, just like we were supposed to do." As soon as the students emerged into a rec area behind the Westside Middle School, just outside Jonesboro, Arkansas, a concussive sound erupted. At first the youngsters assumed it was firecrackers. But when chips of concrete and dirt began flying and several students fell wounded, there was pandemonium. "Oh, my God, this isn't a fake. Run! Run!" Pittman remembers someone yelling. But not all could run fast enough. The rampage, lasting less than a minute, killed four girls—two 12-year-olds and two 11—and teacher Wright, 32, who died shielding Pittman from harm.

The source of the carnage was no less shocking: Mitchell Johnson, then 13, and his pal Andrew Golden, just 11. Calculatedly, the boys had staged a false fire alarm to lure their school-mates outside, then, from woods a hundred yards away, had crouched in full camouflage gear and opened fire with semiautomatic hunting rifles. At their sentencing five months after the mayhem, Johnson trembled as he said, "I thought we were going to shoot over their heads. We didn't think anybody was going to get hurt." Judge Ralph Wilson sentenced both boys to juvenile detention until they turn 21. But at present, Arkansas has no juvenile facilities for youths older than 18, so Johnson may be released in four years, Golden in fewer than six. "The punishment," Judge Wilson lamented, "will not fit the crime."

Two months after the Arkansas debacle, tragedy struck again at a high school in Springfield, Oregon. This time a freshman named Kip Kinkel, then 15, stepped into the Thurston High cafeteria wearing a cow-boy hat and with a rifle propped against his shoulder. As in Arkansas, students mistook the first bursts for fire-crackers; after all, it was school election day, and stu-dents often held showy displays to win votes. But Kinkel was deadly serious. He killed two students, Ben Walker, 16, and Mikael Nickolauson, 17, and wounded 22 oth-ers. The shooting ended only when Jacob Ryker, 17, shot in the chest, saw his girlfriend Jennifer Alldredge, 17, bloodied by a bullet, and with the help of others, tackled Kinkel as he attempted to reload. "I saw she got hit, and I went for it," says Ryker. "Enough's enough."

That is precisely how most Americans felt after Kinkel discharged his 51 rounds from a semiautomatic rifle and two pistols. Jonesboro and Springfield were only the lat-est communities to see their public schools turned into killing fields. (The horror roll includes Pearl, Mississippi; West Paducah, Kentucky; and Edinboro, Pennsylvania.) What was particularly chilling was the seeming ordinari-ness of the perpetrators. In Jonesboro, both boys had been adequate students without serious discipline prob-lems. In Springfield, Kinkel had until his early teens been a cheerful kid; his parents, whom he allegedly shot to death earlier that day, are remembered by townspeople as devoted to him. (Kinkel will be tried as an adult on four counts of aggravated murder.) "People have been wanting to marginalize the places that have this hap-pen," says Springfield's fire chief, Dennis Murphy. "But this is Middle America. This is you."

The Kinkels, both language teachers, put Kip and sister Kristin on their '96 Xmas card.

A fence at Thurston High School (below) became an impromptu memorial site.

A member of the wrestling team, the hero, Ryker (comforted by his proud Navy-diver father Robert), recovered fully from his wounds.

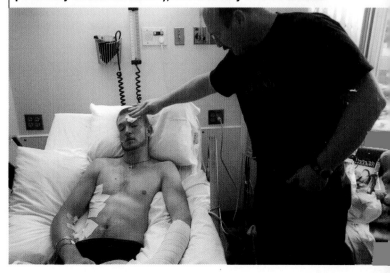

Giving Peace a Chance

After 30 years of fratricidal conflict, Northern Ireland signs onto ending the 'Troubles'

At one point during the two trying years that George Mitchell spent shuttling to Belfast to broker peace between Protestants and Catholics in Northern Ireland, the former U.S. Senate Majority Leader's wife had a miscarriage. So, when his wife delivered a boy in October 1997, Mitchell regarded the birth as a sign of hope. "I had my staff find out how many children were born in Northern Ireland on the same day," he says. "There were 61. I began to think, 'Will those 61 children have the same chance for success that I hope for my son?'"

A hopeful "maybe" became possible on Good Friday, April 10. Following 32 hours of almost nonstop wrangling and repeated telephone prodding from President Clinton, representatives of eight Northern Irish political parties signed an historic agreement, one which could bring peace after three decades of violence that has cost 3,200 lives. According to the pact, ratified in May by voters in Northern Ireland and the Republic of Ireland, Northern Ireland's 1.6 million citizens will no longer be governed by Britain but will manage their own affairs through a new elected assembly of Catholics and Protestants. Perhaps most important, the accord puts unprecedented pressure on terrorists on both sides of the religious divide to surrender their weapons.

Almost immediately the peace proved fragile, with two bombs exploding over the summer. The August incident was the single worst tragedy in 30 years of the "Troubles," claiming 28 lives and injuring 220. But thanks to the accord, all parties to the conflict condemned the carnage—including the Irish Republican Army. And the peace effort received a high-profile boost in October when two of its architects, Catholic John Hume and Protestant David Trimble, were awarded the 1998 Nobel Peace Prize.

Political rivals David Trimble and John Hume joined U2's Bono at a pro-peace concert.

Action Governor

A former wrestling bad guy, Jesse 'the Body' Ventura, upsets the political pros and takes over the Minnesota statehouse

So there he'd be, the brutish, menacing figure—or as menacing as anyone can be in a feather boa—taunting the good guys and whipping up the crowd to a state of ecstatic fury. He and his rival would grapple in the ring, pretending to do all sorts of violence to each other. Finally the loudmouthed meanie would haul himself up on the turn-buckle, pause, with a broad smirk to the crowd, and flatten his hapless opponent. In November, beefy former pro wrestler Jesse Ventura relied on similar flourishes to dispose of two formidable adversaries—the Republican and Democratic contenders (the latter the son of Hubert Humphrey)—to get himself elected governor of Minnesota. Dismissed early on as a flake by the political establishment, Ventura, 47, ran on Ross Perot's Reform party line with a shoestring budget, spending only $300,000 and accepting no donations of more than $50. An ex-Navy SEAL with the heart of a social moderate-to-liberal and the mind of a fiscal conservative, he won in part because he articulated voters' concerns in a straightforward way. But Ventura, who in private dotes on his horse-breeder wife of 23 years and their two children, also benefited from a brilliantly gonzo campaign, which included airing quaintly unslick TV ads that featured a Jesse action figure taking on Special Interest Man. "Finally," said one constituent, "we have a governor who knows how to execute a flying head scissors." Only in America.

A villain supreme (clonking Hulk Hogan in 1984), he became a people's hero.

With a Name like Stein...

Controversy erupts when the Vatican taps a Jewish-born Carmelite nun for sainthood

During canonization, her tapestry was hung at St. Peter's Basilica.

In the end, it took the child of a priest to make a saint of Edith Stein—who in October became the only Jewish-born person to be so honored in modern times. The process was set in motion in 1987 when 2-year-old Teresia Benedicta McCarthy of Brockton, Massachusetts, lay comatose in a Boston hospital, dying of liver failure after she had swallowed a potentially lethal dose of Tylenol. Her father, the Rev. Emmanuel Charles McCarthy, a Roman Catholic priest in the Eastern rite (a church that in some cases ordains married men), responded to the emergency by asking friends and relatives to pray to Stein.

A prominent German-Jewish intellectual who converted to Catholicism at age 30 in 1922, then 11 years later joined the Carmelite order as Sister Teresa Benedicta of the Cross, Stein was gassed by the Nazis at Auschwitz in 1942. Father McCarthy and his wife had honored her memory in the naming of the youngest of their 13 children who was born 42 years to the day after Stein's death. Now, as her family prayed, the little girl initially slipped closer to death. But four days later, a mystified doctor wrote on her chart, "This child has made a remarkable recovery." Four days after that, she went home "healed," says her father.

In 1997, after 10 years of study, debate and testimony by medical experts, the Vatican declared that the recovery of Benedicta McCarthy, now 13, was a miracle attributable to Edith Stein's intercession. This was the final step before her canonization by Pope John Paul II at a mass in St. Peter's Square. A decade earlier, the pontiff had proclaimed her "beatified," calling Stein "a daughter of Israel who remained faithful, as a Jew, to the Jewish people and, as a Catholic, to our crucified Lord Jesus Christ."

His summation underscores the controversy that swirls around Stein. The church asserts that, while serving with the Carmelites in Holland, she was rounded up and sent to her death at Auschwitz in retaliation for the Dutch bishops' criticism of the Nazis. Many Jews disagree. "She had been registered [as a Jew], she had been told to wear the yellow star," says James Baaden, 39, an American rabbinical student who is writing a biography of Stein. "The Nazis proceeded with her exactly as they intended to with all Jews." Thus the canonization brought the charge that the church laid claim to the Holocaust for its own purposes.

No one, however, seems to dispute Stein's goodness. Born on Yom Kippur in 1891 to Orthodox Jews, she studied history and philosophy at three universities, and became one of the first women in Germany to receive a Ph.D. Though Stein never explained her journey from agnosticism to Catholicism, her niece Susanne Batzdorff, 77, says, intriguingly, "Her conversion followed hard upon some romantic disappointments." But Batzdorff also marvels, "It's not every Jewish family that has a saint in their midst."

Benedicta McCarthy (in 1997) has no memory of her "miraculous" recovery.

A Cancer Cure?

Judah Folkman's promising lab results with mice point toward a potential breakthrough

It wasn't the sort of treat that most kids would have treasured, but it meant a lot to young Judah Folkman. On Saturday afternoons his father, Jerome, a rabbi in Columbus, Ohio, would often take him along on his visits to hospitalized members of his congregation. "Judah was exposed to the suffering of others," recalls his brother David, "but also to what science could do for patients who have little hope." Now 65 and a researcher at Children's Hospital in Boston, Folkman has offered hope to the world: His pioneering work with lab animals could lead to a breakthrough in curing cancer. For more than 30 years, Folkman labored far out of the limelight. While mainstream cancer researchers concentrated on directly attacking tumors, he found ways to cut off the blood supply that allows tumors to grow. Then, working with Dr. Michael O'Reilly in Boston, Folkman discovered two natural agents—angiostatin and endostatin—that seem to rid mice of cancer without any side effects. Ironically, many colleagues had for years made light of his work. "A weaker person would have collapsed and gotten out," says Dr. Vincent DeVita, director of the Yale Cancer Center. But Folkman is a tenacious workaholic. At 8, already bent on a medical career, he toiled late into the night in his basement chemistry lab. When his grandfather offered him a Jeep as a bar mitzvah gift, he asked instead for a powerful microscope. In high school his science project won an award when he kept a rat's heart beating outside its body for over 30 minutes. "His hobby is his work, and his work is his hobby," his wife, Paula Prial (with whom he has two grown daughters), once observed. Folkman, who also teaches at his alma mater, Harvard Medical School, remains cautious about his possible oncological coup. "If you have cancer, and you're a mouse," he says, "we can take good care of you."

Hartman's "nickname was 'the Glue,'" said *SNL* creator Lorne Michaels. "He kind of held the show together."

Only the Surface Glittered

Behind Phil and Brynn Hartman's smiles was a badly tattered marriage

How the 10-year marriage of one of Hollywood's most amiable celebrities could end in a bloody murder-suicide was a question that vexed friends and fans last May after comedian Phil Hartman had been fatally shot in his sleep by his wife, Brynn, who then orphaned the couple's two young children by shooting herself in a bedroom of their $1.4 million Encino, California, house. What made the tragedy more puzzling was that, on the surface at least, the Hartmans' marriage was as robust as his career. The Canadian-born Hartman, 49, was an enormously talented and popular performer—lauded for his stinging impressions of Bill Clinton and Frank Sinatra on *Saturday Night Live,* for the goofy characters he voiced on *The Simpsons* and for his role as the pompous anchorman on the NBC comedy *NewsRadio.* While Hartman worked, Brynn, a former model, raised their son Sean, 9, and daughter Birgen, 6. Says Todd Red, a bartender at Buca di Beppo, where the Hartmans had recently celebrated Brynn's 40th birthday: "They always seemed happy."

Yet Hartman, a master mimic, just may have been playing another role. His relationship with Brynn, his third wife, was far more troubled than their public appearances suggested. Friends say that Brynn, who had jettisoned her own acting plans, was volatile and insecure about her husband's fame, while Phil, an outwardly genial man, was often sullen and withdrawn in private. Lawyer Steven Small, a pal of Hartman's, says the comic once told him, " 'I go into my cave, and she throws grenades to get me out.' " That combustible mix was undoubtedly aggravated by Brynn's substance abuse problems. A recovering alcoholic and cocaine user, she had recently resumed drinking after a decade of near-sobriety and had been in and out of rehab. Several days before the homicide, Brynn—who had been taking an antidepressant that can cause violent outbursts if mixed with alcohol or drugs—began drinking and using cocaine again. She had confided to at least one pal that she wanted out of the marriage. Others say it was Hartman who was giving up. "This," notes a TV producer who knew the couple, "was not a happy household." As stipulated in the Hartmans' wills, their children moved in with Brynn's married sister Katherine Kay Wright, 29, who lives in Wisconsin. Friends can only shake their heads in disbelief. Says Rita Wilson, Tom Hanks's wife: "Now two children are left without the two most important people in their lives, and with a lifetime of confusion."

Birgen (above, left) and Sean joined their folks at a 1996 AIDS benefit. Hartman had talked about moving out of Encino (the scene of the tragedy, below) and retiring to Catalina Island.

Reborn in Time To Die

Despite her conversion, rehabilitation and a plea from the Pope, murderer Karla Faye Tucker is executed

Karla Faye Tucker was that rarest of death row inmates: a white, articulate, attractive female who openly avowed her guilt and remorse. From her cell in Huntsville, Texas, she became a lightning rod in the stormy debate over capital punishment once her cause was taken up by an unlikely coalition of liberals opposed to the death penalty and evangelicals moved by Tucker's professed rebirth as a Christian. Joining them in the campaign to spare her life was the brother of one of her victims and Pope John Paul II. But Texas law does not allow life sentences without the possibility of parole, and granting Tucker clemency would have made her eligible for release in five years, a prospect that outraged other relatives of the two people she had helped murder in 1983. So on February 3 at 6:45 p.m., Tucker, 38, became the second woman in the U.S. to be executed since the Supreme Court's 1976 reinstatement of the death penalty.

Just moments before being injected with a lethal mix of three drugs, a dry-eyed and calm Tucker said, "I'm going to go face-to-face with Jesus."

The child of a broken home, Tucker was shooting heroin by age 10 and working as a prostitute at 13. On June 12, 1983, shortly after midnight, Tucker, then 23, and her live-in boyfriend, Danny Garrett, 37, a Houston bartender, wound up a three-day bender of drugs, alcohol and sex by bursting into the home of a biker to steal some motorcycle parts. Finding Jerry Dean, 27, in his bedroom, Garrett smashed his head with a hammer, and Tucker then grabbed a pickax and struck him 20 more times. (Later she bragged that she got a "nut"—street slang for orgasm—with each blow.) Cowering under the bedsheets was Deborah Thornton, 32, who begged not to be killed. Tucker responded by sinking the pickax into her shoulder; Garrett then finished the job. Almost from the time of her arrest, Tucker expressed regret about her role in the two gruesome murders. Soon she began helping fellow inmates find their own faith, and in 1993 she married a prison minister. Seconds before her death, Tucker said, one last time, "I am so sorry."

Waging the Fight of His Life

Michael J. Fox confronts a cruel foe—Parkinson's disease—with courage and pragmatism

As Michael J. Fox and wife Tracy Pollan pulled up to the Beverly Hilton for the 1998 Golden Globe Awards, the actor realized he was in serious trouble. Outside, photographers stood poised to greet the ABC sitcom star, but Fox, 37, was in no shape to greet them. Like so often lately but for the first time at such a public moment, his left arm and leg were shaking uncontrollably. Behind the limo's darkened windows, Pollan, 38, began squeezing Fox's hand and massaging his foot. But for the tremors fully to subside, the couple would have to wait for his medication to kick in. Fox asked the driver to circle the block once. Then a second time. And a third. "He probably thought I was nuts," says Fox with a faint smile. "But I just couldn't get out of the car and let my arm go or mumble or shuffle."

That was in January, at a time when Fox was keeping a secret he was not ready to share with anyone save a tight circle of family and friends. By November he was ready to go public with some difficult news. Through an interview with PEOPLE, Fox let his fans know that he has been battling Parkinson's disease for seven years. A progressive degeneration of the central nervous system that is characterized by tremors and muscle stiffening, the disorder ultimately renders some patients unable to walk, talk or care for themselves. Worse, it has no known cause or cure. But Fox—best known as *Family Ties*'s Alex P. Keaton and as the whizbang hero who speeds *Back to the Future* in three films—is not one to bask in self-pity. "I'm not crying 'What a tragedy' because it's not," he says. "It's a reality, a fact." One, he acknowledges, that was becoming increasingly difficult to hide, despite a grab-bag of tricks he has devised to conceal the symptoms. "I can touch something and stop the tremors for about 15 seconds, or I can move around," he says. "I've done interviews where I've walked the entire time, and later the writer describes me as nervous." To help control milder symptoms, he takes the drug Sinemet. To eliminate radical tremors, he underwent a brain operation two days after taping the season finale of *Spin City*.

While his illness has yet to impede his success (at that Golden Globe ceremony, he was named Best Actor in a Comedy Series), it has rearranged his priorities. Abandoning his film career, Fox has returned to the steadier schedule of a TV series. "Moving to the rhythms of the business clearly made no sense to me," he says. "I needed to live my life for my family and myself." These days, Fox focuses on the good in his life: how much he loves reading science books to his son Sam, 9; the delight he takes in watching his 3-year-old twin daughters, Aquinnah and Schuyler, play dress-up. Since he can no longer play the hockey he has loved since childhood, he takes long walks. "The biggest thing," says Fox, "is that I can be in this situation and still love life as much as I do."

"He's truly remarkable," says Pollan. "He lives the moment. And the moment is good."

Shepard's mom and dad, an oil-rig inspector stationed in Saudi Arabia, spoke to the press.

Young, Gay and Murdered

College freshman Matthew Shepard falls victim to a brutal hate crime

Judy and Dennis Shepard had appealed publicly for a peaceful, dignified service. It seemed the least they could give their son Matthew, 21, a slight, 5'2" college student who had met his grisly fate, police say, at the hands of two young men who brutally beat him, tied him to a fence and left him for dead, seemingly because he was gay. But by the time he was buried 10 days later, Matthew had become something more than his parents' son—a martyr whose slaying served as a brutal reminder of the human capacity for hatred and violence. As a result, some 400 mourners overflowed the pews of St. Mark's Episcopal Church in the prairie town of Casper, Wyoming, while

500 more listened on speakers in adjoining rooms and in a church next door; uncounted others tuned in on the radio. Then there were the protesters—more than a dozen flew in from Kansas and Texas—standing outside, one holding a hand-scrawled placard reading GOD HATES FAGS. Anne Kitch, an Episcopal priest and the wife of Matthew's cousin, eulogized: "He struggled to fit into a world that is not always kind to gentle spirits."

Certainly it was not kind to Matthew Shepard. Late on the evening of October 6, a Tuesday, he stopped at a Laramie bar called the Fireside Lounge, near the University of Wyoming, where he'd just begun his freshman year. Unable to find any schoolmates to join him, he

soon found himself in conversation with Russell Henderson and Aaron McKinney, both 21 and high school dropouts, who were sharing a pitcher of beer. After Shepard had confided that he was gay, police say, the two men lured him outside and into a truck belonging to McKinney's father. The men, according to McKinney's girlfriend Kristen Price, told Shepard they were gay.

Then things turned ugly. Shepard was beaten with the butt of a .357 Magnum pistol, police say, as the two drove to a remote bluff east of town. There they tied Shepard to a buck fence, and, as he pleaded for his life, they bludgeoned him, stole his wallet and black patent-leather shoes and left him for dead. Some 18 hours later, UW freshman Aaron Kreifels took a spill on his mountain bike. Standing up, he saw what he thought was a scarecrow hanging on a fence—until he noticed the human hair. "I realized, 'Oh, my God, it's a person!'" recalls Kreifels. Shepard was taken to a hospital in Fort Collins, Colorado, where five days later he died from his head injuries.

Police subsequently charged McKinney and Henderson with first-degree murder, which in Wyoming can carry the death penalty. Their girlfriends, who allegedly hid Henderson's bloody clothes and failed to report the crime, are charged as accessories to murder after the fact, which is punishable by up to three years in prison.

Shepard had been majoring in political science at UW, his father's alma mater. Friends say he hoped to pursue a public service career, perhaps working for human rights causes. In Laramie, Shepard had found acceptance in a group called the Lesbian, Gay, Bisexual and Transgendering Association. On the last night of his life he had attended a meeting to plan for Gay Awareness Week, just five days away. The sad irony is that Shepard's professed aim to "better humanity" may have been achieved by his death. The viciousness of the crime, which sent shock waves across America, prompted President Clinton to decry Shepard's attackers as "full of hatred and full of fear," and ignited numerous rallies and protests. "Judging from the world's response," Reverend Kitch told mourners in Casper, "Matt will have made a difference in the lives of thousands."

Matthew (above) had built up his self-esteem by acting in community theater in Casper.

The suspects were Henderson (below left), an Eagle Scout, and McKinney, a troublemaker.

"I can't stop crying." said Ellen DeGeneres, who attended a D.C. vigil with Anne Heche to support legislation against hate crimes.

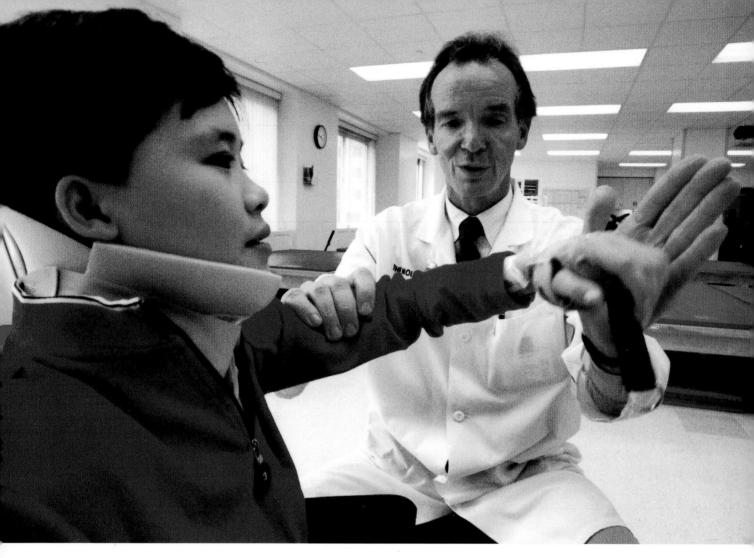

An Indomitable Refusal to Quit

Chinese gymnast Sang Lan may never walk again, but she looks to the future with hope

The traffic in and out of the second-floor hospital room was hardly run-of-the-mill. Leonardo DiCaprio slipped through a back entrance at New York City's Mount Sinai Medical Center to make an unbilled cameo. Celine Dion arrived to perform an a cappella rendition of her *Titanic* hit "My Heart Will Go On." President Carter hand-delivered a stuffed bear; Hong Kong action-movie star Jackie Chan paid a call; and President Clinton and Vice President Gore each sent letters. But even with all that, Chinese gymnast Sang Lan, 17, had to be a real-life Pollyana to find a silver lining in the tragic fall that on July 21 shattered her hopes of winning Olympic gold and instead left her dreaming of, at best, just walking again. Yet only two months after breaking her neck during a routine, warm-up vault at the 1998 Goodwill Games, Sang declared, "It's okay if I can't use my legs because there are so many things that I can still do."

Summoning heroic optimism, determination and her infectious

Spinal cord expert Ragnarsson (top) called her spirit "quite amazing."

smile, Sang has made remarkable progress. During a 13-week stay at Mount Sinai, she took the discipline and tenacity that had helped her become China's 1997 national vaulting champion and applied it to her rehabilitation. Each day from 9 a.m. to 4:30 p.m, she performed a rigorous physical therapy regimen that focused

on strengthening the muscles she still controls in her arms, shoulders, neck, elbows and wrists. "Some movements are hard," Sang allowed. Then she added with a quick smile, "Gymnastics is harder." As she made headway, Sang was reunited with her parents, whom she hadn't lived with since she left home for gymnastics school at age 8. Her father, Sang Shisheng, a government worker, uses a Chinese expression to describe Sang's unyielding resolve: "She's very tough. She can eat bitterness."

By the time she left the hospital in late October, Sang could feed herself, comb her hair, write her name and maneuver a manual wheelchair. Dr. Kristjan Ragnarsson, chairman of the hospital's department of rehabilitation, said that though her hands and legs remain totally devoid of sensation, Sang "has an excellent chance of becoming self-sufficient." (She feeds herself, for instance, with the help of a glovelike splint that, when fitted with a spoon, she digs into her food and raises to her mouth. The same device enables her to brush her teeth, dial a phone and use a pencil.)

While Sang's medical costs are covered by USA Gymnastics and the Goodwill Games, a private group has raised a nearly six-figure fund from family, friends and the public to help handle her housing, food and interpreter costs. She and her mother, Chen Xiufeng, a factory worker, are living at a friend's Manhattan apartment while Sang continues physical therapy at the Rusk Institute of Rehabilitation; and within a year they hope to return to China. For the future, Sang is studying English and planning one day to attend college either here or in her homeland. Gina Liu, vice president of the Chinese Gymnastics Association, has offered Sang an apartment and a job as her secretary in Beijing. Whether Sang goes that route or not, the former Olympic aspirant has her eye on a far bigger prize: walking again. Encouraged by actor Christopher Reeve, who also paid her a visit, she says, "I believe that day will come."

Woman on the Verge: Part II

A domestic dispute lands Farrah Fawcett in court, testifying reluctantly against boyfriend James Orr

"I really don't want to do this," Farrah Fawcett sobbed as she took the witness stand in August to discuss her troubled relationship with producer-director James Orr. Seven months earlier, Fawcett, 51, told Los Angeles police that Orr, 45, had beaten her at his mansion. Five days later, they issued a joint statement calling the fight "a small misunderstanding." But the dried blood, scratches and abrasions on Fawcett's body spoke of something crueler, and, in the wake of the O.J. Simpson case, prosecutors now feel compelled to pursue domestic complaints. Fawcett told jurors that a series of January spats had culminated with her slamming a fireplace poker on Orr's bed (with him in it) and breaking windows. She said that he, in turn, had hit her with a bar stool and smacked her head on the ground. Two days later she struck Orr's car and house windows with a baseball bat. Orr, who produced *Father of the Bride,* was found guilty of dating battery; he was sentenced to three years' probation and 100 hours of community service. It was only the latest, bloodiest mess in the life of *Charlie's* (fallen) *Angel.* Since she and Ryan O'Neal ended their tempestuous, 17-year love match in February 1997, Fawcett has been accused of shoplifting, appeared disoriented on TV and backed out of appearances to promote her latest film, *The Apostle.* As for Orr, the worst may be over: The couple split up before the trial.

Letourneau (in court last February) feels her latest child is a "gift from God."

"Mary didn't take my childhood," says Fualaau (in Paris). "I gave it away."

The Teacher and the Pupil

A strange story gets stranger as Mary Kay Letourneau defiantly has a second child with her child lover

As a teacher, Mary Kay Letourneau was praised as someone who could see things through the eyes of a child. Now one wonders whether she can see things any other way. As a married mother of four, Letourneau, 36, had already made headlines in 1997 when she'd had a baby by Vili Fualaau, her 13-year-old former student. In November 1997, at her sentencing for child rape, she vowed, "I give you my word, it will not happen again." After a defense psychiatrist had testified that Letourneau suffered from bipolar disorder, a form of manic depression that often leads to reckless behavior, Judge Linda Lau sentenced Letourneau to 7½ years, suspending all but six months on the condition that the Washington state resident enter a treatment program for sex offenders, take medication for her disorder and end all contact with her underage lover. But within days of her release on January 2, Letourneau stopped taking the medication and began defying her sexual-deviancy counselor. A month later, after she was discovered in her car with Fualaau, Judge Lau ordered Letourneau back to prison to finish her sentence. By then, she was already pregnant again by Fualaau. Hours after the hospital delivery of the baby, a second daughter, Letourneau was returned to the Washington Corrections Center for Women. This time the improbable couple made no pretense of contrition. "It's unfair. I want Mary to be with me and the kids," Fualaau, now 15, told PEOPLE. Together, they collaborated with a ghostwriter on *Un Seul Crime, L'Amour* (Only One Crime, Love), which earned a reported $250,000 advance in France after U.S. publishers showed little interest. Fualaau maintains they didn't do the book for money, and in fact Letourneau can't be paid since state law bars felons from profiting from works based on their crimes. "We wanted to tell the real story of our relationship," says Fualaau, who first met Letourneau when she was his second-grade teacher. By their own account, the sexual encounters didn't begin until Fualaau was in Letourneau's sixth-grade class. For now, Fualaau's mother and an aunt are the primary caretakers of the couple's daughters. Letourneau's ex-husband Steve, 35, has moved to Alaska with their four children, who range in age from 5 to 14. Fualaau hopes eventually to attend art school. And Letourneau, a friend says, believes the two will someday marry. But unless an appeal wins her a shorter sentence, she will remain in prison until 2005.

Mary Letourneau
Vili Fualaau

un seul crime, l'amour

In their book, Fualaau claims that he, not Letourneau (in court in 1997), initiated sex: "It was my idea."

The Wrath of Hurricane Mitch

The deadliest natural disaster to hit Central America this century batters Honduras

The name was deceptively benign, more appropriate to a favorite uncle than to an agent of mass destruction. But when Hurricane Mitch tore through Central America in late October, it left in its wake a toll far greater than the estimated $4 billion in property damage that downed power and phone lines, ruptured water and sewer pipes, flooded the seasonal banana crop and transformed verdant tourist hideaways into gray-brown wastelands. More than 10,000 people died, most of them in Honduras, with hundreds of thousands more at risk from disease. Another 10,000 were missing, and millions were homeless.

In response, U.S. citizens stepped in to help their battered neighbors.

Hungry children at an orphanage in Tegucigalpa welcome relief supplies from the U.S.

Mission Impossible

The Pope preaches freedom in Fidel Castro's Cuba

Harry Oakes Jr., a search-and-rescue expert from Oregon, paid his own way.

A 126-member unit of the U.S. Navy's Second Naval Construction Brigade helped clear a dirt road to an isolated village in central Honduras. Globe-trotting relief workers waded through rubble in the capital city of Tegucigalpa to deliver vital food supplies. Relief workers arrived to search ravaged areas for signs of life beneath the mounds of debris. In the U.S., school kids spearheaded drives to gather shippable supplies.

Political celebrities of both stripes used their clout to make Americans aware of the need for help. Former President George Bush, 74, took to the airwaves to encourage Americans to dig into their pockets and assist the relief effort. Second Lady Tipper Gore, 50, led a 10-person delegation to hard-hit areas of Honduras and Nicaragua, taking supplies, comfort—and her camera. And President Clinton pledged $80 million in humanitarian aid to complement the million-plus tons of clothes, food, bottled water and medicine sent by U.S. agencies overwhelmed by people phoning in to offer help. "Never in our history have we had this volume of calls—100,000 in a five-day period," said Ann Stingle of the American Red Cross. Clearly, the tragedy brought out the best in all Americans.

Even for a Pope as peripatetic as John Paul II—he has visited 116 countries during his 20-year reign—this trip promised to be a standout: a five-day visit to the island of Cuba. Unimaginable, really, the thought of the conservative pontiff, 77, one of communism's greatest and most persistent decriers, engaging in an intimate tête-à-tête with the revolutionary Fidel Castro, 71, one of communism's greatest and few remaining champions. Yet there they were, on January 22, huddled together behind closed doors in Havana for almost an hour. When they emerged to pose for pictures and exchange gifts, Castro's hand gently guided the Pope, who, suffering the early stages of Parkinson's disease, walked with a shuffle. Both seemed determined to find common ground. Upon his arrival the Pope said this was a "happy and long-awaited day," then called upon the U.S. to end its 37-year economic embargo of trade-starved Cuba. "Holy Father," the Cuban leader warmly responded, "we feel the same as you do about many important issues of today's world." But as John Paul II traversed the length of the island to conduct four open-air Masses, it was plain that more than an ocean separated the two men. The Pope chastised the Cuban régime for its human rights record and prohibition of Catholic education, and denounced the common practice in Cuba of premarital sex, abortion and divorce. But then, at year's end, Castro issued a conciliatory decree declaring December 25th a national holiday. Except for a provisional observance in connection with the Pope's visit, this was the first official celebration of Christmas in Cuba since 1968.

El Jefe greeted His Holiness after he had celebrated Mass for several hundred thousand in Havana's Revolution Square.

All Their Lovin' Was Real

Linda McCartney's long, winding journey ends with family by her side

As celebrity marriages go, theirs was an anomaly—a limelighted couple who couldn't bear to be apart even after 29 years of marriage. "The only 11 days we ever did not spend the night together," Paul McCartney told PEOPLE in 1993, "was when I got put in jail in Japan for pot." They were again briefly separated in 1997 when Paul flew to London for his knighting ceremony. Linda, who had been diagnosed with breast cancer in 1995, was undergoing chemotherapy at the time and couldn't travel. So, to commemorate the event, she bought him a silver pocket watch and engraved it in her own hand: "To Paul, my knight in shining armour—Linda."

On April 17, in a real-life *Love Story* ending, the woman Paul calls "my girlfriend, lover and wife" died in his arms at 56 during a specially arranged horseback-riding holiday at their 150-acre ranch in Tucson, Arizona. Six months later, Paul, 55, told the *London Daily Mail* that, though he knew a week before her death that she was fading, he didn't tell her: "I didn't think she'd want to know." He said he had been coping with his loss by talking with a therapist and recording the final track of Linda's new solo album, *Wide Prairie*. "If I work, I want to work on stuff that's connected with Lin," he said. "It just seems more meaningful."

In the public mind, Linda Eastman was pegged primarily as the pretty blonde from a tony New York City suburb who snagged the cutest Beatle, then lent her undistinguished vocal talents to Wings, the band that Paul put together two years after the Beatles' 1970 breakup. But Linda was also a talented photographer, who made a mark shooting black-and-white portraits of rock stars. Her work has been collected in five books and shown at countless galleries. She was a dedicated vegetarian who crafted two bestselling cookbooks and developed a successful line of meatless frozen foods.

Undeniably, though, her greatest passion was her family. Of their four children (one of whom Linda had brought from a prior marriage), Paul told the *Daily Mail,* "We wanted to care for them ourselves." Determined to give them an "ordinary" life, they sent the children to local schools near their home in Sussex, England. "Because neither of us were big into education and didn't get degrees, we weren't desperate for our kids to do that," Paul said. "All we wanted was for them to have big hearts." The parents' success was evident in September when the surviving clan gathered to see middle sister Mary, 29, a photographer like her mom, exchange wedding vows with TV producer Alistair Donald. As for the secret of Linda and Paul's enduring passion, Sir Paul says simply, "We just fancied each other. That was the whole root, the whole essence of our love."

Describing her 1969 London wedding (the scene afterward, below), Linda said, "The bride wore a big smile." After her death, Sir Paul cried and told a friend, "Wasn't she wonderful?"

They attended the 1997 premiere of one of his symphonic works at Royal Albert Hall.

Just days before Linda's final trip to the U.S., this last picture of her was shot at the McCartneys' East Sussex home by their photographer daughter Mary.

Forsaking a tux,
ROBIN WILLIAMS
wore a collarless jacket
that he joked was from
"Armani's Hasidim
collection."

PARTY ANIMALS

OSCARS

They say that show folk will flock to the opening of anything, including, or especially, an envelope. If the year seemed like one long marathon awards-cast and post-ceremony gala, then its photo journal made for a sizzling and competing Star Report. Party after party saw scarlet women, hunks in shorts (well, Michael Richards anyway), tumescent egos, exposed backs and, aptly, necklines that plunged like the mid-'98 Dow. "In about three years," cracked Conan O'Brien at one of the shows, "I think we're looking at an all-nude Emmys."

The glitz just kept on coming, and 1998 wound up as glam as it gets. Or as good, for Helen Hunt anyway, who in a dazzling triple took home statuary at the Golden Globes, the Oscars and the Emmys. After all, the very point of being a star is to shine. For the whole party animal kingdom, it's a chance to stride down red carpets and bask in the glitter of the strobes and the adulation of fans. Sure, it's work, but even for the non-nominees and the losers, partying is such sweet sorrow.

"It's been such an amazing ride. I think **ALEC** is speechless tonight," said **KIM BASINGER**, with the affectionate **BALDWIN** at Mortons.

OSCARS

The Oscars

70TH ANNUAL ACADEMY AWARDS

(Presented March 23, 1998)

Picture: *Titanic* Actor: **Jack Nicholson,** *As Good as It Gets* Actress: **Helen Hunt,** *As Good as It Gets* Supporting Actor: **Robin Williams,** *Good Will Hunting* Supporting Actress: **Kim Basinger,** *L.A. Confidential* Director: **James Cameron,** *Titanic* Original Screenplay: **Ben Affleck** and **Matt Damon,** *Good Will Hunting* Adapted Screenplay: **Brian Helgeland** and **Curtis Hanson,** *L.A. Confidential* Music, Original Song: **"My Heart Will Go On,"** *Titanic,* **James Horner** and **Will Jennings** Honorary Award: **Stanley Donen,** director (*On the Town, Singing in the Rain, Pajama Game, Seven Brides for Seven Brothers*) Cinematography: *Titanic* Original musical or comedy score: *The Full Monty,* **Anne Dudley** Original Dramatic Score: *Titanic,* **James Horner** Documentary: *The Long Way Home* Animated Short: *Geri's Game* Costume: *Titanic* Film Editing: *Titanic* Sound: *Titanic* Art Direction: *Titanic* Visual Effects: *Titanic*

DREW BARRYMORE's fresh-as-a-daisy do was "my idea," said the star of *Ever After.*

BRAD PITT (stag for the big night) skipped the ceremony to party elsewhere with Robert De Niro.

For the Olympic ice-skating star **TARA LIPINSKI,** the Oscars were "so different."

MATT DAMON, whooping it up with buddy-since-boyhood **BEN AFFLECK** (right), got some great advice—"Just try and enjoy the moment"—from mom Nancy, who was also his date.

Here they're chummy, but sometimes full-figured **KATE WINSLET** went through hell or high water during *Titanic*'s filming, like weathering barbs from director **JAMES CAMERON,** who dubbed her Kate-Weighs-a-Lot.

"You can't be an actor and not dream of this moment," exulted **HELEN HUNT,** looking like a winner in a Grace Kelly-inspired, ice-blue Gucci gown.

The Globes

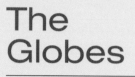

55TH ANNUAL GOLDEN GLOBE AWARDS

(Presented January 18, 1998)

MOTION PICTURES   Drama: *TItanic*
Actor, Drama: **Peter Fonda,** *Ulee's Gold*
Actress, Drama: **Judi Dench,** *(Her Majesty)*
Mrs. Brown   Musical or Comedy: *As Good*
as It Gets   Actor, Musical or Comedy:
Jack Nicholson, *As Good as It Gets*   Actress,
Musical or Comedy: **Helen Hunt,** *As Good*
as It Gets   Supporting Actor: **Burt**
Reynolds, *Boogie Nights*   Supporting
Actress: **Kim Basinger,** *L.A. Confidential*
Director: **James Cameron,** *TItanic*   Screen-
play: **Matt Damon and Ben Affleck,** *Good Will*
Hunting   Score: **James Horner,** *Titanic*
Song: **"My Heart Will Go On,"** *Titanic*
TELEVISION   Drama Series: *The X-Files*
Actor, Drama Series: **Anthony Edwards,** *ER*
Actress, Drama Series: **Christine Lahti,**
Chicago Hope   Musical or Comedy
Series: *Ally McBeal*   Actor, Musical or
Comedy Series: **Michael J. Fox,** *Spin City*
Actress, Musical or Comedy Series:
Calista Flockhart, *Ally McBeal*   Miniseries
or Movie Made for Television: *George*
Wallace   Actor, Miniseries or Movie
Made for Television: **Ving Rhames,**
Don King: Only in America   Actress, Minis-
eries or Movie Made for Television:
Alfre Woodard, *Miss Evers' Boys*   Support-
ing Actor, Series, Miniseries or Movie
Made for Television: **George C. Scott,**
12 Angry Men   Supporting Actress,
Series, Miniseries or Movie Made for
Television: **Angelina Jolie,** *George Wallace*

Always ready to help a lady, **DUSTIN HOFFMAN**
brings up the rear of the pale-green Givenchy that
Good Will Hunting nominee **MINNIE DRIVER**
said may "end up in a museum."

RUPERT EVERETT and **JULIA ROBERTS** (with newly lightened hair, in Todd Oldham) were both nominated for *My Best Friend's Wedding*—but both were left to cool their heels at the altar.

Presenter **JADA PINKETT SMITH** was still in a clingy Badgley Mischka seven months before she and Will Smith welcomed son Jaden. Her fashion secret: "Every day my husband tells me I'm beautiful."

"I'll be 58 next month. But I feel like an 8-year-old," **PETER FONDA** fessed up as he effusively congratulated fellow victor and old *Easy Rider* pal **JACK NICHOLSON.**

GOLDIE HAWN and **KURT RUSSELL** arrived with **JENA MALONE,** a nominee for Hawn's directing debut in the TNT movie *Hope.*

EMMYS

Frasier's **KELSEY GRAMMER** (with wife Camille, in a silver Richard Tyler) said his Magic 8 Ball predicted the show's fifth Emmy win.

The Emmys

50TH ANNUAL PRIME-TIME EMMY AWARDS
(Presented September 13, 1998)

Drama Series: *The Practice*   Comedy Series: *Frasier*
Variety, Music or Comedy Series: *Late Show with David Letterman*
Miniseries: *From the Earth to the Moon*   Lead Actor, Drama Series:
Andre Braugher, *Homicide: Life on the Street*   Lead Actress, Drama:
Christine Lahti, *Chicago Hope*   Lead Actor, Comedy Series: **Kelsey Grammer,** *Frasier*   Lead Actress, Comedy Series: **Helen Hunt,**
Mad About You   Lead Actor, Miniseries or Special: **Gary Sinise,**
George Wallace   Lead Actress, Miniseries or Special: **Ellen Barkin,** *Before Women Had Wings*   Supporting Actor, Drama:
Gordon Clapp, *NYPD Blue*   Supporting Actress, Drama: **Camryn Manheim,** *The Practice*   Supporting Actor, Comedy: **David Hyde Pierce,** *Frasier*   Supporting Actress, Comedy: **Lisa Kudrow,**
Friends   Supporting Actor, Miniseries or Special: **George C. Scott,** *12 Angry Men*   Supporting Actress, Miniseries or Special: **Mare Winningham,** *George Wallace*
Individual Performance, Variety or Music Show:
Billy Crystal, *The 70th Annual Academy Awards*

Hosting the Oscars earned **BILLY CRYSTAL** an Emmy—and a congratulatory call from Johnny Carson.

After the show, **WHITNEY HOUSTON** told hubby **BOBBY BROWN,** "I want Taco Bell."

In keeping with his alter ego's habit of making an eye-catching entrance, **MICHAEL RICHARDS** turned up in shorts festooned with pom-poms and an Armani tuxedo top.

After a series win for *The Practice*, **DYLAN McDERMOTT** (with wife Shiva Afshar) vowed to "stay out late and celebrate."

"I was always told I'd never make it in TV," said *The Practice*'s **CAMRYN MANHEIM.** But the actress's Emmy offers irrefutable evidence against the naysayers. Manheim giddily accepted her win "for all the fat girls."

The Daytime Emmies

25TH ANNUAL DAYTIME EMMY AWARDS

(Presented May 15, 1998)

Drama: *General Hospital* Talk Show: *The Rosie O'Donnell Show* Game Show: *The Price Is Right*

Actor: **Eric Braeden**, *The Young and the Restless*

Actress: **Cynthia Watros**, *Guiding Light*

Supporting Actor: **Steve Burton**, *General Hospital*

Supporting Actress: **Julia Barr**, *All My Children*

Talk Show Host (tie): **Oprah Winfrey** and **Rosie O'Donnell** Lifetime Achievement Award: **Oprah Winfrey**

EMMYS

"I'm on a lucky streak," said **CYNTHIA WATROS** (bussed by castmates **FRANK GRILLO** and **PETER HERMANN**).

"I don't like having to compete," said **O'DONNELL,** resplendent in a Dale Richards pantsuit. Nonetheless, Rosie the Riveting certainly seemed to love her award.

With some assistance from Mom, *General Hospital*'s **REBECCA HERBST** stitched together her own tourniquet-tight gown.

X-Filer **DAVID DUCHOVNY** and wife **TÉA LEONI** mingled with an alien life-form: presenter **GARRY SHANDLING.**

COURTNEY THORNE-SMITH didn't get a statuette—or dinner. "I'm very busy holding in my stomach," said the *Ally McBeal* costar, who was poured into a champagne-colored Escada.

"I'm the only chick here who didn't borrow her dress," boasted *3rd Rock from the Sun*'s very down-to-Earth **KRISTEN JOHNSTON.** Instead, the Space Girl raided her own closet for her elegant—and gravity-defying—strapless Isaac Mizrahi gown.

The SAG Awards

THE ACTOR

4TH ANNUAL SCREEN ACTORS GUILD AWARDS
(Presented March 8, 1998)

FILM   Actor: Jack Nicholson, *As Good as It Gets*   Actress: Helen Hunt, *As Good as It Gets*   Supporting Actor: Robin Williams, *Good Will Hunting* Supporting Actress (tie): Kim Basinger, *L.A. Confidential*, and Gloria Stuart, *Titanic*   Motion Picture Cast: Mark Addy, Paul Barber, Robert Carlyle, Deirdre Costello, Steve Huison, Bruce Jones, Lesley Sharp, William Snape, Hugo Speer, Tom Wilkinson, Emily Woof, *The Full Monty* TELEVISION   Actor, Movie or Miniseries: Gary Sinise, *George Wallace*   Actress, Movie or Miniseries: Alfre Woodard, *Miss Evers' Boys* Actor, Drama Series: Anthony Edwards, *ER*   Actress, Drama Series: Julianna Margulies, *ER*   Actor, Comedy Series: John Lithgow, *3rd Rock from the Sun*   Actress, Comedy Series: Julia Louis-Dreyfus, *Seinfeld* Ensemble, Drama Series: Maria Bello, George Clooney, Anthony Edwards, Laura Innes, Alex Kingston, Eriq LaSalle, Julianna Margulies, Gloria Reuben, Noah Wyle, *ER*   Ensemble, Comedy Series: Jason Alexander, Julia Louis-Dreyfus, Michael Richards, Jerry Seinfeld, *Seinfeld*

SAG

The unsinkable **CELINE DION** made a splash in an iceberg-blue Halston sheath.

DEANA (*Did I Shave My Legs for This?*) **CARTER** flaunted her smooth gams in a Richard Tyler-designed gown—and ankle cast.

The Grammys

40TH ANNUAL GRAMMY AWARDS

(Presented February 25, 1998)

Record of the Year: **"Sunny Came Home," Shawn Colvin**
Song of the Year: **"Sunny Came Home," Shawn Colvin**   Album of the Year: *Time Out of Mind,* **Bob Dylan**   New Artist: **Paula Cole**
Male Pop Vocal: **"Candle in the Wind 1997," Elton John**   Female Pop Vocal: **"Building a Mystery," Sarah McLachlan**   Pop Vocal by a Duo or Group: **"Virtual Insanity," Jamiroquai**   Traditional Pop Album: *Tony Bennett on Holiday,* **Tony Bennett**   Rock Song: **"One Headlight," Jakob Dylan**   Male Rock Vocal: **"Cold Irons Bound," Bob Dylan**   Female Rock Vocal: **"Criminal," Fiona Apple**   Rock Vocal by a Duo or Group: **"One Headlight," Wallflowers**   R&B Song: **"I Believe I Can Fly," R. Kelly**   Male R&B Vocal: **"I Believe I Can Fly," R. Kelly**   Female R&B Vocal: **"On and On," Erykah Badu**
R&B Vocal by a Duo or Group: **"No Diggity," Blackstreet**   Rap Solo: **"Men in Black," Will Smith**   Rap Performance by a Duo or Group: **"I'll Be Missing You," Puff Daddy and Faith Evans, featuring 112**   Hard Rock Performance: **"The End Is the Beginning Is the End," Smashing Pumpkins**   Metal Performance: **"Aenema," Tool**
Alternative Music Performance: **"OK Computer," Radiohead**

Sparkling poet **JEWEL** did not need iambic pentameter to voice a forecast of her fate: "I don't think I'll win."

Country casual **LORRIE MORGAN** and hubby Jon Randall joined the jeans-and-leather brigade but left their cowboy hats at home.

She wasn't nominated for a Grammy, but teen singer **LEANN RIMES** was still blooming in her silver-strapped Chanel.

The CMAs

52ND ANNUAL COUNTRY MUSIC AWARDS

(Presented September 23, 1998)

Entertainer: **Garth Brooks**   Male Vocalist: **George Strait**   Female Vocalist: **Trisha Yearwood**   Single: **"Holes in the Floor of Heaven," Steve Wariner**
Album: ***Everywhere,* Tim McGraw**   Vocal Group: **Dixie Chicks**   Vocal Duo: **Brooks & Dunn**   Music Video: **Faith Hill, "This Kiss"**   Horizon Award: **Dixie Chicks**   Song: **"Holes in the Floor of Heaven," Billy Kirsch, Steve Wariner**
Event: **Patty Loveless with George Jones, "You Don't Seem to Miss Me"**

DIXIE CHICKS Martie Seidel, Natalie Maines and Emily Erwin were really smokin' at the Sony records bash after their triumph.

PEOPLE'S CHOICE

"I'm so excited being here. It's my first awards show, so I feel like I'm in a movie right now," cooed **JENNA ELFMAN,** dancing chic-to-chic with *Dharma* costar **THOMAS GIBSON.**

Lifetime Achievement winner **GOLDBERG WHOOPI**s it up with daughter Alexandra Martin and movie box office hero **HARRISON FORD.**

Winning "is a huge honor," said *Veronica's Closet*'s **KIRSTIE ALLEY,** "especially since I have a show mostly about underpants."

People's Choice

24TH ANNUAL PEOPLE'S CHOICE AWARDS
(Presented January 11, 1998)

TELEVISION   Female Performer: **Oprah Winfrey**   Male Performer: **Tim Allen**   Female, New Series: **Kirstie Alley,** *Veronica's Closet*   Male, New Series: **Tony Danza,** *The Tony Danza Show*   New Series (tie): *Dharma & Greg* and *Veronica's Closet*   New Dramatic Series: *Brooklyn South*   Dramatic Series: *ER*   Comedy Series: *Seinfeld*   Daytime Dramatic Series: *Days of Our Lives*   Female Musical Performer (tie): **Whitney Houston** and **Reba McEntire**   Male Musical Performer: **Garth Brooks**
MOVIES   Actor: **Harrison Ford**   Actress: **Julia Roberts**   Comedy: *Liar Liar*   Drama: *Jerry Maguire*   Lifetime Achievement Award: **Whoopi Goldberg**

JANE KRAKOWSKI— better known as Elaine, *Ally McBeal*'s busybody secretary—shows off her busty body in a Ben de Lisi concoction.

Lion King's **JULIE TAYMOR** called her win "dessert for the whole evening."

The Tonys

52ND ANNUAL TONY AWARDS
(Presented June 7, 1998)

Play: *Art,* Yasmina Reza   Musical: *The Lion King*   Actor, Play: Anthony LaPaglia, *A View from the Bridge*   Actress, Play: Marie Mullen, *The Beauty Queen of Leenane*   Actor, Musical: Alan Cumming, *Cabaret*   Actress, Musical: Natasha Richardson, *Cabaret*   Featured Actor, Play: Tom Murphy, *The Beauty Queen of Leenane*   Featured Actress, Play: Anna Manahan, *The Beauty Queen of Leenane*   Featured Actor, Musical: Ron Rifkin, *Cabaret*   Featured Actress, Musical: Audra McDonald, *Ragtime*   Choreography: Garth Fagan, *The Lion King*   Revival, Play: *A View from the Bridge*   Revival, Musical: *Cabaret*

"I'm nervous, and I'm glad to be here," said **NATASHA RICHARDSON**, who nabbed a kiss from her husband, **LIAM NEESON** (and also a Tony).

The Academy of Country Music Awards

Country couple **FAITH HILL** and **TIM McGRAW** had multiple reasons to smile at this year's ceremony. They took home four statuettes for their duet "It's Your Love." And they let the world know that Faith was pregnant with their second child.

The American Comedy Awards

How else could **JERRY LEWIS** thank the writers, producers, directors and agents who voted for his Lifetime Achievement Award but with a yuck?

The MTV Movie Awards

Perhaps **JIM CARREY** thought he was one lucky devil for winning the evening's Best Comedic Performance award. Then again, maybe the accolades for *Liar, Liar* just went to his head.

The American Music Awards

Host **DREW CAREY** (with **WEIRD AL YANKOVIC,** left) didn't feel out of his depth. "It's not like sky-diving or anything," he said. "It's only an awards show."

The VH1 Fashion Awards

Leave it to **CHRIS ROCK** to make a fashion statement with little more than a big fig leaf. "I'd like to thank my designer—God!" he said.

The MTV Video Music Awards

MADONNA took six trophies plus heat from Hindus for wearing Vaishnava tilak, holy facial markings representing purity, while performing the provocative "Ray of Light," the Video of the Year.

Leo-mania swept from Paris to New York City (inset), where Greg Kinnear observed, "He's becoming the Beatles right before our eyes."

Hollywood's Hot, Hot Supernova

After *Titanic* and *Iron Mask,* Leonardo DiCaprio
lands in a lifetime of loot and idolotry at age 23

Ever since his 1991 debut as a homeless adolescent on the ABC sitcom *Growing Pains,* Leonardo DiCaprio has kept in touch with his TV father, actor Alan Thicke. At Christmas 1997, as usual, Thicke opened a card to find the familiar "Leo" signature. But this time there was a newsy, handwritten update. "I expect to be busy promoting this little film I'm in," it read. "It's about a boat." The vessel in question, of course, was *Titanic,* a juggernaut that grossed more than $1 billion worldwide—and that was before it hit the home video market.

Feted in Paris, mobbed in London and nearly trampled in Tokyo, the then 23-year-old DiCaprio has been riding a crest of adulation known to very few mortals. "I've never seen a frenzy like this," marveled Sherry Lansing, chairwoman of Paramount, which cofinanced *Titanic.* "I don't know what to relate it to: the Beatles, Elvis, Frank Sinatra in his heyday." To be sure, DiCaprio's blockbuster '98 hat trick—he played a scrappy young artist in *Titanic,* both a hard-hearted king and a

He cavorts in Manhattan with two pals, magician David Blaine and actor Lukas Haas.

dashing swashbuckler in *The Man in the Iron Mask* and a spoiled movie star in Woody Allen's *Celebrity*— proved his virtuosity. But his box office performance was positively boffissimo, with *Titanic* and *Iron Mask* tied one week for the No. 1 spot in movie grosses. Says Kate Winslet, now 23, his *Titanic* costar: "Leo is absolutely awesome."

All of this must come as something of a shock to DiCaprio, whose career got off to a shaky start in Los Angeles when, at 5, he was booted off the set of *Romper Room* for being disruptive. (His mother, a onetime legal secretary, and his father, a self-described "old hippie" who produced underground comic books, separated when he was an infant but raised him together.) Even after TV commercials led to guest gigs on *Roseanne,* what had impressed the casting agents still didn't work

In Paree, he partied after the *Titanic* premiere with model Eva Herziqova.

on the girls. "He was kind of a dork," recalls Susanna Mejia, a high school classmate.

Indeed, the early DiCaprio specialized in decidedly unsexy roles. They did stretch him as an artist—he got an Oscar nomination as a mentally impaired boy in 1993's *What's Eating Gilbert Grape*—but painted him as quirky. Then, after a romantic breakthrough in 1997's *Romeo and Juliet,* he climbed aboard a sinking ship and, voilà! In the U.S., crazed fans made waves at the box office, seeing *Titanic* 30 and 40 times. They also keelhauled bestseller lists by snapping up four books about Leo. On the Internet, devotees could get a Leo fix by accessing any of the estimated 500 Leo-related Web sites. And everywhere the movie opened, there were the screaming hordes of worshipping adolescents. "His existence," explained one awestruck French teen, "has forever changed my life."

Such fame carries a heavy price. In March, Leo drew fire for pulling a no-show at the Academy Awards ceremony (where *Titanic* swept up 11 Oscars). "Why should he go? He wasn't nominated," argued his mother, Irmelin. Three days later, Leo unsuccessfully filed suit to stop *Playgirl* magazine from publishing

11 "nonconsensual nude photographs of Plaintiff"—stills from his 1995 film *Total Eclipse*. (The in-the-buff pix hit newsstands in September.) And needless to say, every time the club-hopping Leo is spotted around town chatting up a beautiful woman—Naomi Campbell, Mia Sorvino, Alanis Morissette—it's headline news. (Actually, the only woman to have come close to claiming DiCaprio all to herself was L.A. model Kristin Zang, whom he dated for 15 months.) "Wherever he walks, there is a gang of people, 10 deep, who want a piece of him," says a colleague. "Leo never really wanted to be what he has now unfortunately become."

On the other hand, Leo now has a career that commands upward of $20 million a picture. Carefully controlling his screen image, DiCaprio took his time selecting a follow-up to *Titanic* and finally settled on the role of a wandering backpacker in search of utopia in *The Beach*. The shooting takes him to relatively isolated Thailand—where, if he's lucky, he'll find peace and quiet before the next tidal wave of Leo-mania.

At the Tokyo Film Festival, as everywhere else on the planet, his ship came in.

The Ace of Clubs

With four wins as a rookie, South Korea's Se Ri Pak has stolen the spotlight from Tiger What's-His-Name

A gifted sprinter and shot-putter, Si Re Pak decided at 14 to focus exclusively on golf. Her father, a building contractor, became her coach and mentor—and proved a tough one at that. To help her conquer her fears, he once made her spend an evening alone in a cemetery. "And if she made mistakes, I would holler and break clubs," says Joon Chul. The payoff came when Pak started winning tournaments in her native South Korea—30 amateur events in four years—then joined the U.S. tour last January. Though all of 20 and a first-year player in the Ladies Professional Golf Association, Pak went on to win four tournaments, including a thrilling play-off victory at the U.S. Open. On the golf course, Pak is trailed by a noisy contingent of worshipful Koreans and Gen Xers. Off the links, the tunnel-visioned star lives alone in Orlando. "Right now golf is first, and my life is second," she says through an interpreter. "If I really concentrate for the next 10 years or so, then when I'm 30, I will live like a human being."

Après golf the shy Pak hangs out, mainly with her beagle Happy (above).

In Amarillo, Winfrey taped five shows a week before audiences of about 300 people and generated some $250,000 in local business.

Another Year of Ubiquity

Texas jurors had no beef with Oprah Winfrey, who also ventured *Beloved*

n many ways the joys of Amarillo were lost on Oprah Winfrey. During the six weeks she stayed in the Texas Panhandle city, defending herself in a $10 million libel suit brought by a group of cattlemen, the talk show empress raced between courthouse and make-shift TV studio, crashed in an unluxurious bed-and-breakfast, dodged fans who chased her even into bathroom stalls—and gained weight. By the beginning of jury deliberations, Winfrey, 44, was seriously bummed out. "Maybe it'll be a hung jury," she told a friend, "but I'm ready to lose." This time the woman with the Midas instincts was wrong. After mulling over the case for less than six hours, the jury delivered the verdict: Winfrey was not liable for any damages to the Texas cattle industry—despite her glib on-air comment during Britain's 1996 mad cow disease scare that the prospect of its spreading to the U.S. "just stopped me cold from eating another burger. I'm stopped."

Almost nothing else has stopped the indefatigable Oprah this year. Already America's most powerful talk show host, book critic and all-round inspiration, Winfrey also produced several noteworthy projects for the small screen, *The Wedding* among them, and one megafilm, *Beloved*. The latter provided Winfrey with a juicy vehicle for her return to the big screen: the unglamorous role of Sethe, a steely-eyed runaway slave haunted by painful memories. Though the film received a mixed reception from critics and performed disappointingly at the box office, Winfrey herself received glowing reviews and strong intimations of an Oscar nomination.

The film's attendant hype landed America's Golden Girl (*Forbes* puts her worth at $675 million) on the cover of everything from TIME to *Vogue* to INSTYLE, looking spectacularly svelte and uncommonly glamorous. Winfrey was also the media-dubbed mogul of the year, earning "most influential" accolades from *Vanity Fair* and *TV Guide* and the No. 1 spot on ENTERTAINMENT WEEKLY's annual list of the Power 101 in showbiz. Some might think the Winfrey franchise a bit overextended—now she's even peddling a line of "boyfriend pajamas"—and the supernova does seem a bit removed from the just-one-of-the-girls who made her name looking, sounding and feeling like her fans. But, hey, as Stedman Graham, 46, her fiancé of six years, told his beloved, "This is your year."

In *Beloved* she starred with Kimberly Elise (left) and Thandie Newton.

A slender Oprah turned up for the *Beloved* premiere, proving that the once-chunky Queen of Empathy can do fashionable and sexy too.

The touchy-feely model dad credits therapy for healing his family post-divorce. McGwire has pledged $1 million a year to children's charities—more than a tithe from his three-year, $28.5 million contract.

A Truly Grand Slam

Mark McGwire and Sammy Sosa turn a *mano a mano* slugfest into a hugfest

He could just have gift-wrapped a really nice tie. But Mark McGwire had something special in mind for his father's 61st birthday. On Labor Day, with one mighty lash of his 33-oz., 34 ½-inch bat, the St. Louis Cardinals slugger bashed his 61st home run of the season, tying the most glamorous record in sports and turning dentist John McGwire into the happiest dad in St. Louis's Busch Stadium save possibly for Mark himself. The next night, again facing the Chicago Cubs, the Bunyanesque 6'5", 250-lb. McGwire hit a vicious line drive that shattered Roger Maris's 37-year-old record.

As he had the night before, McGwire, 34, marked the moment by scooping up his 10-year-old son, Matt (who lives with McGwire's ex-wife in California but often visits his father in St. Louis and fills in as a Card batboy). Next, he climbed into the stands at Busch Stadium and tearfully embraced members of the late Maris's

family. As baseball fans were drying their eyes and thinking it doesn't get any better than this, Chicago Cub Sammy Sosa, 29, hustled in from the outfield to give McGwire a hug—a perfect moment in a perfect rivalry between two superstars who defy the modern stereotype of the overpaid, spoiled, selfish, pro athlete.

Then, 116 hours later at Chicago's Wrigley Field, Sosa transformed a Milwaukee pitch into his own 62nd homer. After his victory lap the Dominican Republic's pride and joy had a message for McGwire: "Mark, you know I love you. It's been unbelievable. I wish you could be here with me today." McGwire had a response: "Imagine if we're tied at the end. What a beautiful way to end the season." Though the ending wasn't quite so tidy—McGwire finished with 70 homers to Sosa's 66—the legend of their gentlemanly joust will prove as enduring as their eye-popping stats.

McGwire clasped Sosa midseason (top) and later, with his final swing, wacked No. 70.

Pop's Newest Diva

At 23, Natalie Imbruglia has risen from Down Under to make a splash on both sides of the Atlantic

With her angelic blue eyes, flirtatious pout and cover-girl good looks, Natalie Imbruglia is the favorite daydream of many a teenage boy. She's also the preferred listening of many a teenage girl. The Australian native's debut album, *Left in the Middle,* with its angst-ridden lyrics and heartbreak vocals, sold nearly 5 million copies; her first single, "Torn," dominated the airwaves for almost a year. Moreover, her climb to the top of the charts in both Britain and the U.S. (assisted by a prerelease appearance on *Saturday Night Live*) came just months after she had cut the album. No less amazing is that this is a second successful career for Imbruglia, who is only 23. Raised in a Sydney suburb, she first achieved fame at 17 costarring on the Aussie soap opera *Neighbors.* "I used to go clubbing, drinking," she says of those days. "I was a little big for my breeches." Some detractors say that hasn't changed. Described by *The Times* of London as a "supersonic tyrant," Imbruglia also struck a sour chord in the music world when she rejected a song written for her by British pop star Robbie Williams. Linked romantically with a variety of men, including a Scottish member of Parliament and a millionaire businessman, Imbruglia is a diva whose future promises many intriguing turns.

A Most Lucrative Education

Singer Lauryn Hill triumphs with an album fusing hip hop, reggae and gospel sounds

She's from a loving, stable family and a tony New Jersey suburb, but Lauryn Hill is not your typical suburban girl. For one thing, she was the single mother of two. For another, she was a triple-threat talent whose acting, singing and rapping skills earned her TV and movie roles and a Grammy award by age 23. And last fall her debut solo album, *The Miseducation of Lauryn Hill,* climbed to the top of *Billboard*'s pop chart within a week of its release. (You *do* know that Hill wrote and produced the whole thing, right?)

Back when Hill was only dreaming of glory, her mother (an English teacher) and father (a computer consultant) told their daughter that they would support her ambitions—provided Hill put her school work first. "She kept up her end of the bargain," says mother Valerie. Enough so, in fact, that Hill eventually earned admission to Columbia University, which she attended for two years before embarking full-time on a music career. By then she had landed parts Off-Broadway, on TV, in *As the World Turns,* and on the big screen, in Steven Soderbergh's *King of the Hill.* She had also sung in the 1993 Whoopi Goldberg comedy *Sister Act II: Back in the Habit* and helped secure a recording contract for The Fugees, a three-member rap group she'd formed with two high school chums. (The Fugees' 1996 album *The Score* went on to sell 17 million copies.) As she approached marriage to Rohan Marley, a former college football player who is the father of her children and the son of reggae legend Bob Marley, Hill saw more movies and more music in her future.

Hill is so close to her parents that she and her man, Marley, often crash with her folks—though she has her own pad down the road.

Boy, Oh Boy!

The Backstreet Boys go platinum with a rollicking debut album and a tour that drives teens wild

The countdown to the Backstreet Boys' Las Vegas concert had begun, and the pop quintet's fans were having another manic attack at the MGM Grand Hotel. It had been an hour since their beloved Boys—Howie Dorough, A.J. McLean, Nick Carter and cousins Kevin Richardson and Brian Littrell—had dashed through an alley entrance to shower and change before the show, but the hundreds of hysterical pubescent girls refused to go away. "I love Nick!" one shouted. "For Nick I'll die." Kids say the darnedest things. Especially those whom the Backstreet Boys kept running into on their 42-city summer tour. Not since New Kids on the Block ruled the charts in the late '80s have a gang of five heartthrobs made so many teenyboppers swoon. The band formed and got its start playing at the Backstreet Market in Orlando in 1993, then caught on in Europe before hitting it big in the U.S. After topping the singles pop chart four times, they no longer struggle for recognition. They do, however, wrestle with the hazards of excessive popularity. During a show in Canada, more than 50 fans had to be treated by paramedics after a horde of people surged toward the stage. The group faced its only major crisis when doctors discovered that a congenital hole in Brian's heart had enlarged to dangerous proportions. He obtained medical permission to postpone surgery, then had a successful operation—but only after the tour had concluded.

The group (from left): Carter, Dorough, Littrell, McLean and Richardson.

Adams is excited about having "a miniature me" by soccer-star fiancé Beckham.

Scary calls her dancer husband, Gulzar, "lovely."

Dicey Spice

Ginger quits, then tries on a Princess Di act!
Scary and Posh are preggers! You go, girls!

In the world of sugar and spice, everything was not quite nice. On May 31, Geri "Ginger Spice" Halliwell, 25, quit the Spice Girls, the British pop-tart posse, with a vague statement blaming "differences between us" and concluding, "P.S., I'll be back." As prepubescent girls around the globe went into mourning, rumors flew that Halliwell (a former topless model) had a) lost a Girl Power battle with Melanie "Scary Spice" Brown, 23; b) was mentally and physically exhausted; c) had tired of the Spice capades and was seeking a career change. Five months later, when Halliwell resurfaced publicly to sing at Prince Charles's 50th birthday bash in London, all traces of trashy Ginger had vanished. Goodbye, two-toned hair, pancake make-up, dark talons and plunging necklines. Hello, strawberry-blonde chignons, natural freckles, close-cut nails and a wardrobe befitting a modest college girl or her hero Margaret Thatcher. To complete her stunning transformation, Halliwell began raising money for breast cancer research and took on the $1-a-year post of goodwill ambassador to the U.N. Population Fund, with plans to to kick off her reign by promoting a British essay competition about

population control.

Umm, speaking of which—two of the remaining four Spice Girls are in the family way. Yup. Both Brown and Victoria "Posh Spice" Adams, 24, are due sometime around March. The father of Adams's child is her fiancé, soccer player David Beckham, 23, who made humiliating headlines in June for kicking an opponent, leading to his expulsion from a World Cup match and perhaps England's elimination. In September, Brown wed the father of *her* child, dancer Jimmy Gulzar, 26, who performed on the Spice Girls' world tour, which wrapped that month. Some sticks-in-the-mud grumble that such behavior is unworthy of mega- role models and could precipitate a spate of out-of-wedlock pregnancies. Others predict that the group's pregnant pause may become permanent. But the Girls are, like, completely unimpressed. "We are sisters and love each other and love being together as a band," the group insisted in a joint public statement. "We plan to continue on, perhaps adding two new members to the Spice family."

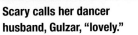

The artist formerly known as Ginger (left) emerged from her makeover (right) looking posher even than Posh.

JUDGE
JUDY SHEINDLIN

A No-Nonsense Bench Warmer

All rise—including the ratings—for TV's smart, sassy and currently supreme jurist, Brooklyn's own Judy Sheindlin

Judy Sheindlin metes out justice, often with the subtlety of a catapult meting out boulders. When British punk rocker Johnny Rotten tried to mouth off in her TV courtroom, she silenced him with a curt "I'm going to show you the door." To a woman whose case involved a crushed hat, she advised, "You better get a life, madam." When she's sick of waiting for a straight answer, she barks in a rasping Brooklyn accent, "Baloney! Baloney! Baloney!" If Sheindlin's justice seems extreme, it is also extremely entertaining—which is why her syndicated half-hour show, *Judge Judy,* is enjoying such strong ratings. In only its second season, it already has topped *The People's Court* (which provided the model for adjudicating small claims cases, with up to $5,000 awarded in damages). Ed Koch, who presently presides over *The People's Court* and who as mayor of New York City appointed Sheindlin to the Manhattan bench in 1982,

says of his rival, "She has a greater tendency to lecture." But bluster aside, Sheindlin rules from the heart. Says the show's bailiff, Petri Hawkins-Byrd, who served under Sheindlin in New York City: "She truly gives a damn about these people."

Sheindlin, 55, relies on the gut instinct she developed while raising five children and hearing 20,000 family court cases. From her father, a dentist, she got her salty language—including the title of her 1996 book on family courts, *Don't Pee on My Leg and Tell Me It's Raining.* The only female in her class at New York Law School, Sheindlin brought up her first two kids while working as a prosecutor in family court. Her 12-year first marriage to a lawyer foundered in part on career issues ("He viewed my work as something to keep me busy, like bridge"). Second husband Jerry Sheindlin, a supreme court judge in The Bronx who brought three children to their marriage in 1978, doesn't make that mistake. "What you see," he says, "is what you get." To wit: a petite powerhouse, part Harry Truman, part Rhea Perlman, who is funny, quick-tempered, bluntly honest—and blessed with what Judy likes to call "people sense."

Divine Write

Seattle's Rebecca Wells scores a blockbuster as U.S. women readers go gaga over Ya-Yas

As the four spirited, unconventional belles of Rebecca Wells's second novel, *Divine Secrets of the Ya-Ya Sisterhood,* make clear, true Ya-Yas love and look out for one another. "The Ya-Yas have become a cult," says a Tennessee member of one of the Ya-Ya Clubs proliferating across America and dedicated to deepening friendships by adopting the loyal, fun-loving ways of the book's characters. Crescendoing word of mouth shot *Ya-Ya,* a so-so-selling hardback in 1996, to the top of *The New York Times* paperback charts. "I think I wrote it because I wanted Ya-Ya sisters of my own," says Wells, a tiny, 40ish actress who got serious about writing after realizing there was a paucity of big roles for petite women. (Just ask Bette Midler, who snapped up film rights.) How does Wells feel about inspiring so many women to smoke, drink and never think? "Well, that's just one part of the book. I say, 'Go, girl.'" Spoken like a true Ya-Ya.

Diary Queen

Helen Fielding's *Bridget* proves a hit on both sides of the Atlantic

British author Helen Fielding wants to get one thing straight: She is *not* the loopy protagonist of her hit novel *Bridget Jones's Diary,* that single, thirtysomething career woman whose neurotic jottings about booze and cigarette intake, staying thin and men have made her a household name on two continents. Unlike Bridget, who winds up in a disastrous affair with her boss, analyzing the fallout over more wine and smokes, Fielding is a single, 39-year-old Londoner who insists, "I don't drink, don't smoke and am a virgin. . . . Yeah, *right*!" Indeed, if the success of her comical *Diary* is any gauge, there may be a bit of Bridget in more women than would care to admit it. Fielding, who worked for 10 years as a BBC-TV producer, discovered her inner Bridget in 1995 when a London paper asked her to write a column based on her satirical first novel, *Cause Celeb.* Now, with a film and a sequel in the works, Fielding wryly reports, "The 'Why aren't you married?' has stopped."

Her free-spirited style trumped the exacting but unenergetic routine of Michelle Kwan.

A Dynamo Who Does It Her Way

After an upset victory at Nagano, rink wunderkind Tara Lipinski turns pro

Three nights earlier she'd skated an inspired short program, during which the only thing bigger than her jumps was her radiant, ear-to-ear smile. But when that still left her in second place, behind Olympic favorite Michelle Kwan, 17, the pundits pretty much wrote off Tara Lipinski as four years away from the gold. Everyone, that is, except the 4'11", 82-lb. Lipinski, who had two surprises in store. First, during the long program in Nagano, Japan, she exuberantly skated right past fellow American Kwan to claim the gold. Then, at the advanced age of 15, the new champ both stunned and angered the skating-world pooh-bahs by announcing her retirement from amateur competition.

Without apology, Lipinski explained that after 12 years of training, which had compelled her and her mom to live far from her Texas-based dad for five years, "it was what's best for me and my family." Besides, she made clear, her goal had been to win a gold medal. Now that she'd been there, done that, it was time to have some fun. Since her "retirement," Lipinski has toured with two ice shows and snagged a host of endorsements that range from the image-enhancing (Tobacco Free Kids) to the lucrative (Chevrolet) and demonstrate a reach that stretches from the glamorous (Barbie dolls) to the nutritious (Campbell's Soup). At sweet 16, she can now indulge her passion for hanging out at malls with her friends without any lingering regrets. "I don't have to worry about the Olympics anymore," she says. "I won."

Golden Ladies

In Miracle on Ice II, the U.S. beats Canada to take home history's first women's Olympic hockey title

Until the '98 Games, many Americans weren't aware that there was such a thing as women's ice hockey. Then the U.S. team took to the rink in Japan. Relying on speed, strength and determination, they polished off China, Sweden, Finland and Japan before facing their true nemesis: Canada. At all four of the earlier women's world championships, the U.S. had lost to the colossus to the north. But in February the 20 U.S. players, who ranged in age from 18 to 31, checked, elbowed and slap-shot their way to glory. "It's everything I thought it would be," marveled forward Alana Blahoski. By claiming the first Olympic gold medal ever to be awarded in the sport, the U.S. women gave a boost to the fast-spreading popularity of women's team sports in general—and, in particular, to one that has actively discouraged females. Said team captain Cammi Granato: "All of a sudden everybody's like, 'I get it. It's cool that you play hockey.'" Even guys joined their fan club. Said Mike Eruzione, captain of the comparably breakthrough, "miracle on ice" U.S. men's winners of 1980: "They are really a pleasure to watch."

Tricia Dunn (right) helps set up Karyn Bye's exultation (top).

Foot Soldier

Sammo Hung's appeal is a mix of heft, deadpan humor and force

With some 140 kung fu movies under his hapkido black belt, veteran actor-director Sammo Hung has no problem executing the three big fights he averages per show as Detective Sammo Law on the tongue-in-cheek CBS cop series *Martial Law.* Harder for the 5'9", 240-lb. Hong Kong-born Hung are the acrobatic antics he must pull off, like spinning on his head atop a table. Though Arsenio Hall was recently added to the cast, it is Hung, 46, with his comedic élan and broken English, who is credited with luring more women than men to the audience. His dialogue coach is his wife, Mina, 33, the 1986 Miss Hong Kong.

Savvy Coed

Keri Russell shines as a sensitive but unsudsy college freshman

Keri Russell doesn't mind being touted as this year's Calista Flockhart, who hit prime-time gold last season on *Ally McBeal.* Just don't compare her title character on the new WB college drama, *Felicity,* to a certain waifish lawyer with a weakness for teensy-weensy skirts. "Girls in real life look a lot more like Felicity," says Russell, 22. They might be looking up to her too. "She's the daughter parents would like to have, the girlfriend boys would like to have," says *Washington Post* TV critic Tom Shales. Not that Felicity is a perfect role model. She picked her college because there was a cute boy she wanted to be near, and she majors in mixed emotions. "She's impulsive," says Russell, a native of Fountain Valley, California, who made her splash in 1996 on *Malibu Shores.* "I have much more clear thinking." If the show should lose favor, Russell, who possesses an unassuming star quality, hints that she might take a cue from Felicity. "College," she says, "is definitely an option."

"As long as he has a blanket and a tiny little mattress, he's happy," says pal Frank Coraci. "He's the most basic guy."

A Funny Man Who Laughs Last

Adam Sandler spins a dumb and dumber movie into critic-proof gold

Isabel Pellerin doesn't think that Adam Sandler is one bit funny. She has never seen him on *Saturday Night Live,* nor has she ever taken in any of his goofball films, which include *Airheads* and *Billy Madison.* "You have seen his movies?" asks Pellerin, who was Sandler's official disciplinarian at New Hampshire's Manchester Central High School from 1980 to 1984. "That's the way he was here." He was always pleasant, she explains, but always fooling around— silly voices, naughty words, frat-boy antics—and that just wasn't conducive to a proper school atmosphere. "I thought he would grow up," she says. "Instead, he grew rich." Big time. Sandler's per-picture asking price is now an

Sandler waxed amorous with *Wedding Singer's* Drew Barrymore and silly with *Waterboy's* Henry Winkler.

estimated $20 million—understandable, given his pair of 1998 successes. *The Wedding Singer,* which opened in February, was a surprisingly romantic $80 million box office hit, while the exuberantly nitwit *The Waterboy* earned $100 million in its first three weeks despite stinging reviews. "Adam has always been criticized by a genera- tion of people who felt confident that when the Next Big Thing happened, they would recognize it," says *SNL* cre- ator Lorne Michaels, who hired San- dler in 1990. "[But] comedy changes and, of course, part of it enrages the previous generation." While Sandler, 32, works hard, friends and family say he is led solely by his inner child. Give the guy an air hockey table (like the one in his two-bedroom, Manhattan bachelor pad), a bunch of old college buddies with whom to watch football and free- dom to leave his dirty clothes on the floor, and the Next Big Thing is content.

With a Bang, Part of Our World Ended

In one season, we bid a sad, soppy adieu to Jerry, Candice, Garry and three sitcoms for the ages

Seinfeld

For months, all anyone seemed to talk about was Jerry, Jerry, Jerry. What was the premise for the final episode (a secret that, unlike the recipe for a nuclear bomb, never leaked)? What would fill *Seinfeld*'s cherished NBC Thursday night slot? (Answer: *Frasier.*) And, absent Jerry, Elaine, George and Kramer, would life have meaning? (Answer: Get a life.) When May 14 finally came, 76.3 million tuned in—a whole lotta people for a show that prided itself on being about a whole lotta nothing. After nine seasons, Seinfeld went out on top, just as real-life Jerry, 44, wanted.

Post-*Seinfeld,* the year's highest-paid entertainer hit the road with a stand-up act that culminated on Broadway with a show aired live on HBO. His new life included a tidy move back to Manhattan and a messy liaison with a newlywed. That's our Jerry.

Murphy Brown

"For the last week I've felt like someone was standing on my chest," Candice Bergen said in May while shooting the final episode of *Murphy Brown.* Then she flashed a wry smile: "Other than that, it's been great." One might say the same of the sharp, smart CBS sitcom, which won 18 Emmys during a 10-season run that saw TV reporter Murphy struggle with everything from alcoholism and idiot bosses to breast cancer. Her 1992 decision to have a child out of wedlock put the fictional newswoman into real-life confrontation with then-Vice President Dan Quayle. Bergen, whose husband, Louis Malle, died in 1995, says that with the show's conclusion, "I'll have a bigger void than some of the others."

Larry Sanders

Seinfeld be damned—some TV viewers thought the bigger tragedy was the demise of HBO's *The Larry Sanders Show* after just six seasons. Hailed by PEOPLE's TV critic as "the funniest series of the decade," the program lampooned late-night talk shows. Although this Susan Lucci of sitcoms will now never snag a Best Comedy Emmy (six straight nominations ended in disappointment), its creator-star, Garry Shandling, 48, continues to rivet attention with a $100 million lawsuit against his former friend and manager Brad Grey and a typically and wildly off-center tell-all *Autobiography of Larry Sanders.*

Shortly after reaching space, mission commander Curt Brown radioed, "Let the record show: John has a smile on his face, and it goes from one ear to the other."

Discovery to Earth: 'Zero G, and I Feel Fine!'

At age 77, Senator John Glenn savors the joys, rigors and challenges of space flight—36 years after he made his historic first orbit

On a clear Florida morning in 1962, some 10 months after Soviet cosmonaut Yuri Gagarin had been hurled into orbit, Marine fighter pilot John Glenn, 40, climbed into a cramped titanium capsule dubbed *Friendship 7* and electrified his countrymen by becoming the first U.S. spaceman to circle the globe. The flight lasted 4 hours and 55 minutes. On October 29, 1998, at Cape Canaveral, Glenn, now 77, was again launched into space, this time with a nine-day agenda of tests to study problems common to the aging process and weightlessness. Back in January, a year from the end of his fourth and final term representing Ohio in the U.S. Senate, he announced his plans to return to space, saying, "I can't help but stand here before you with a real sense of déjà vu." The actual mission seemed like a golden oldie tour, as well. In 1998, as in 1962, Glenn announced his successful liftoff with the words, "Zero G, and I feel fine." And when the people of Perth, Australia, once again turned on their lights to greet the circling astronaut, Glenn declared that the city "looks even better." But other aspects of the two journeys were decidedly different. While Glenn flew solo in 1962, this time he had six shuttlemates, all at least 31 years his junior. Instead of calling the shots, the senator took orders from commander Curt Brown, 42, who was just shy of 6 at the time of *Friendship*'s launch. And when Glenn returned from his 3.6 million-mile journey (which involved circling the Earth 134 times instead of only three), he was welcomed by Annie, his wife of 55 years, his two children and his two grandsons, 16 and 14—the very ages Glenn's two kids were when he first ventured into space. Mission accomplished, Glenn had a message for fellow seniors: "You should run your life not by the calendar, but how you feel."

As both the commander of *Friendship 7* (above) and a payload specialist on *Discovery*, Glenn had the right stuff.

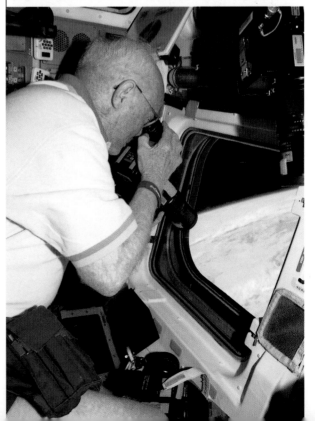

Bond of Love

After the death of an Illinois teen, two ill people find not only new life but each other

The tragedy that cut short the life of Hickerson (above) has made miracles for others.

Just three years ago, Kristin Gabrielson and Chris Nelson were close to death. Both had been desperately sick most of their lives, she with Hodgkin's disease and the aftereffects of radiation therapy, he with a series of ailments that destroyed his liver. Nelson had even prepared himself to die. Then, in January 1995, Meghan Hickerson, 14, a popular cheerleader from Illinois, took a fatal header while out on a church-sponsored ski trip. Though reluctant at first, Meghan's parents agreed to donate her organs. Among the five lucky recipients: Gabrielson, who got new lungs; and Nelson, a new liver. Introduced three months later, through Meghan's parents, the two went on to fall deeply in love. On the third anniversary of their transplants, Nelson, 29, pledged that he and Gabrielson, 29, would marry. "I want," he says, "to live my life with Kristin."

A Star of Self-Help

Iyanla Vanzant's inner voice proves inspiring for others

The journey that landed author Iyanla Vanzant on the bestseller list and made her a spiritual guru among African-Americans began in 1979 with a wake-up call. "The voice of God herself came to me and said, 'Leave here now,'" recalls Vanzant, then just 25 and living in Brooklyn with an abusive second husband. When she took her three children as far as the subway and realized she was penniless, "that voice came again and said, 'Don't give up.'" A stranger paid her fare—and she was on her way. After putting herself through college and law school, Vanzant, 44, struck upon the mix of New Age affirmations, African spiritualism and frank accounts of her own missteps that makes her seven books inspiring—and lucrative.

First Career, Second Effort

Remarried and on TV again, sportscaster Marv Albert is 'just so happy' to be back

In the year since Marv Albert began his court-ordered psychotherapy sessions, there has been much for him to ponder: the exposure of his sex life, which allegedly included a taste for threesomes, women's lingerie and biting; his four-day trial last year on charges of forcible sodomy and sexual assault; and the destruction of his career as one of sportscasting's top play-by-play men, culminating in his firing by NBC and his resignation from cable's MSG. Now, Albert is a new man at 57. In September he married Heather Faulkiner, 40, the ESPN producer who had stood by him throughout the scandal. Albert returned to the microphone on MSG, anchoring its *SportsDesk* half hour and (long-term, post-lockout) pro-

viding play-by-play for the Knicks on MSG's radio network, with TV play-by-play a future possibility. "I think I'm a better person now, though I'm still a work in progress," says Albert, who continues to see a therapist once a week. "While I still have a sense of humor, I'm much more serious about things than I was." He says he talks more to his four grown children, two sportscaster brothers and, of course, the new Mrs.: "Heather and I talk about everything. I never did that before. I always thought that things would work themselves out."

"You have to give someone a second chance," says Faulkiner (with Albert at their wedding, above). Marv began his resuscitation on radio and MSG cable (right).

Better Late Than Never

These rewards, remembrances and releases brought a sense of closure long past due

A Juror Rights a Courtroom Wrong

The Georgia jury deliberated just three hours before convicting Wayne Cservak of molesting Christopher Cools, 13. But the May 1997 verdict didn't sit right with Juror No. 7. "It was a terrible, overwhelming feeling," says Jim Thomas (above), 69, who runs a glue company. So Thomas hired an attorney to appeal Cservak's case. After a judge voided the conviction, citing inadequate representation, Cools recanted. Cservak, 21, who'd served 10 months in prison, was released.

A Civil Rights Pioneer Is Remembered

In the '60s, James Farmer achieved prominence as a Freedom Rider and founder of the Congress of Racial Equality. Then time forgot him—until January, when the President awarded the civil rights giant, 78, the Medal of Freedom, the nation's highest civilian honor.

Never Too Late to Be a Man of Letters

At 98, George Dawson had survived four wives, four siblings, one of his seven children and decades of grueling jobs. Long retired, he still grew and cooked most of his own food, and angled for bass in lakes near his Dallas home. But there was one skill he had never acquired: reading. When a teacher from an adult education program came calling, he decided, "It's time to learn to read." After two years in a literacy class, Dawson, 100, reads at the third-grade level and can recite the alphabet forward—and backward.

Belatedly, a Vietnam Vet Gets His Medal

The first bullet left a gaping hole in his left hand. Two more shots bloodied his left knee and head. But that day in 1966, Bob "Doc" Ingram, 53, continued to attend to the Marines who had fallen into a North Vietnamese ambush. It took a fourth bullet to the groin to knock the medic out. Plainly, the valorous Ingram was deserving of a Medal of Honor, but the paperwork got lost. Finally, in July, the inexcusable lapse was rectified.

His Bravery Saved Nine Lives

As a U.S. Army helicopter pilot in 1968, Hugh Thompson was dispatched to My Lai to help U.S. troops reportedly engaged in a firefight with Vietcong guerrillas. When Thompson instead found nine Vietnamese civilians under attack by more than a dozen GIs, he landed his chopper in a position that halted the fire, then had the villagers airlifted to safety. Now 54, Thompson returned to the massacre site for a ceremony (below) and was finally honored by the Pentagon.

Justice Is Served Three Decades Late

When Vernon Dahmer, a black Mississippi grocer, began collecting poll taxes from his neighbors in 1966 so they could vote, white businessman Sam Bowers decided he had to be stopped. Holding court in a café, Bowers and his men opted for Project Four—Ku Klux Klan code for murder. Days later, night riders firebombed Dahmer's house, killing Dahmer. Four Klansmen went to jail, but not Bowers. Then, in 1994, Bob Stringer came forward. He'd been in the café that day but, at 19, had been afraid to speak up. Thanks in part to his former errand boy's testimony, Bowers, 74, was convicted of the heinous murder. Stringer (left), now 52, joined the Dahmer family for a quiet celebration.

She Directed an Auteur Wedding

Barbra Streisand and James Brolin marry with a backdrop of family, pals and a greenhouse of flowers

It was probably the most beautiful wedding I've been to," said John Travolta of the ceremony that united Barbra Streisand and James Brolin in her Malibu mansion. On July 1, the second anniversary of their first date, Streisand, 56, in a shimmering, crystal-beaded Donna Karan gown and a 15-foot diaphanous veil, walked down an aisle in her formal living room. The 105 guests included her mother, Diane Kind, 89, designer Donna Karan, Travolta's wife, Kelly Preston, and Tom Hanks and his wife, Rita Wilson. "We wanted to be surrounded by people we've loved a long time," says Streisand, who held hands with Brolin, 58, while Rabbi Leonard

Her Pacific-side home was ideal for a wedding. Her first marriage, to Elliott Gould, ended in 1971.

Beerman did the honors. Then, to enthusiastic applause, the newlyweds engaged in "a really incredible kiss," says the groom's sister Sue Desper, a computer engineer.

The couple met when Christine Peters, ex-wife of Streisand's former boyfriend, producer Jon Peters, fixed her up with the 6'4", silver-haired star of *Pensacola: Wings of Gold*. He had been married twice, for 20 years to casting agent Jane Agee and for nearly a decade to *WKRP in Cincinnati*'s Jan Smithers. After Brolin drove Streisand home, they talked until 3 a.m., and he moved in by the end of the year. Brolin fantasized about a quickie "drive-through wedding," but Streisand talked him out of it. When the time came, they did it up in a style befitting the detail-obsessed director. The house was fragrant with 200 lilies of the valley, 500 gardenias, 2,500 stephanotis blossoms and 4,000 roses. Composer pal Marvin Hamlisch conducted a 16-piece orchestra. "Everyone here knows and loves Barbra and particularly knows how she wants everything to be letter-perfect," Hamlisch began in a toast following the ceremony. "Therefore I have been asked by Jim and Barbra to thank everyone who came to this, their third wedding rehearsal." In fact, the script worked flawlessly. "I'm the happiest person in the world," said Brolin. As for the bride: "In all the years I've known Barbra, I've seen her happy, but always with a cloud," said her longtime friend, songwriter Marilyn Bergman. "This time it was a clear blue sky."

After cutting the cake, a radiant Streisand sang to her brand-new husband, "Just when I thought love had passed me by, we met . . ."

Playing the Match Game

Stars and newsmakers who felt ideally suited looked for the union label

Combining two joyous occasions, South African President **NELSON MANDELA** and **GRAÇA MACHEL,** 52, an advocate for international child welfare, married on his 80th birthday outside Johannesburg.

Barefoot **CINDY CRAWFORD,** 32, and club owner **RANDE GERBER,** 36, opted for a casual ceremony on Paradise Island in the Bahamas.

SHARON STONE, 39, created headlines on Valentine's Day by wedding newspaper editor **PHIL BRONSTEIN,** 47, at her Benedict Canyon mansion.

Assignments in war-torn Bosnia and other international hot spots did not stop CNN's **CHRISTIANE AMANPOUR,** 40, and **JAMES RUBIN,** 37, the chief State Department spokesman, from making a happy newsbreak.

Actors **MACAULAY CULKIN,** 17, and **RACHEL MINER,** 17, both received parental permission before saying "I Do" in a 174-year-old Connecticut church.

KATE WINSLET, 23, wed **JIM THREAPLETON,** 25, assistant director of her upcoming *Hideous Kinky,* in England.

A long way from the beach, *Baywatch* star **TRACI BINGHAM**, 30, and musician **ROBB VALLIER**, 28, became Mr. and Mrs. in Ames, Iowa, where Vallier had proposed.

A secret wedding in Las Vegas seemed like a down-to-earth idea for **FRENCH STEWART**, 34, and **KATHERINE LaNASA**, 31. He's an alien in NBC's *3rd Rock from the Sun.* She's a student and his longtime girlfriend.

FOX News reporter **DOUGLAS KENNEDY**, 31, met teacher **MOLLY STARK**, 28, on Nantucket, so they brought their families there for the big day. Douglas is the 10th child of Robert F. and Ethel Kennedy.

"You could see they were truly, truly happy," said Al Roker of his *Today* show cohort **MATT LAUER**, 40, and Dutch model **ANNETTE ROQUE**, 32, after they wed in New York's Hamptons.

In a 13th-century Norman church in the tiny English village of West Wycombe, singer **TORI AMOS**, 34, and **MARK HAWLEY**, 34, a sound engineer, recited their promises.

Marching down the aisle was a piece of cake for actor **TONY CURTIS**, 73, and bride, horse trainer **JILL VANDEN BERG**, 28.

SOLEIL MOON FRYE, 22, and producer **JASON GOLDBERG**, 27, wed in Los Angeles, where she had spent her childhood on television's *Punky Brewster.*

Separation Nation

This ain't Pleasantville: Husbands, wives and significant others turn terminators as old romances fade and new flings take fire

Friends and associates say **BRUCE WILLIS**, 43, and **DEMI MOORE**, 35, fell victim to a common Hollywood affliction—too much time apart. And so Moore's publicist announced that she and Willis were separating after more than 10 years of marriage and children Scout, 6 (left), Rumer, 9, and Tallulah, 4 (not pictured).

Irreconcilable differences claimed **PAULA ABDUL**, 35, and her Los Angeles clothing manufacturer **BRAD BECKERMAN**, 31, after less than two years of wedlock.

JAMES CAMERON, 43, and **LINDA HAMILTON**, 41, met while filming 1991's *Terminator 2: Judgment Day.* They split after Cameron became interested in *Titanic* actress Suzy Amis.

Playboy mogul **HUGH HEFNER**, 71, and his "playmate for a lifetime" **KIMBERLY CONRAD HEFNER**, 35 (with children Marston, 7, left, and Cooper, 6, in '97), separated after an 8½-year union he called "the best time of my life."

She wore his ring, but perky *Friends* star **JENNIFER ANISTON**, 29, and actor **TATE DONOVAN**, 34, were never officially engaged during their 2½-year romance. They called it quits, and she moved on to Brad Pitt.

A country singer and his former Dallas Cowboy cheerleader wife, **TRACY** and **STACIE LAWRENCE,** split after Tracy, 30, was found guilty of domestic battery against Stacie, 28.

Supermodel **LINDA EVANGELISTA**, 33, and actor **KYLE MacLACHLAN**, 39, slowly grew apart after almost six years together. "We'll always remain friends," says the fashion favorite.

MIRA SORVINO, 30, said that although she still loved director **QUENTIN TARANTINO**, 34, "very much," they had reached a mutual decision that "at this point in our lives, we should not be together." So ended 2½ bewitched years.

Eight years of unwedded bliss turned out to be quite enough for **ERIC STOLTZ**, 36, and **BRIDGET FONDA**, 34—even though she once declared Stoltz "the love of my life."

"Our lives are moving in different directions," said **LINDA EVANS**, 55, and **YANNI**, 43, in a joint statement. Pals said Yanni's long tours took too much away from their relationship.

WYNONNA JUDD, 34, sued to end her 1996 marriage to **ARCH KELLEY**, 46, a boat dealer turned househusband and dad to their two kids. Hoping to reconcile, he hung in for the interim at their 500-acre Tennessee farm.

Less than 2½ years after actress **ROMA DOWNEY**, 37, and director **DAVID ANSPAUGH**, 51, wed in Salt Lake City, Downey filed for divorce. Both placed the blame on his depression.

He had once worked as her chauffeur, so it was only fitting for **ROSEANNE**, 45, to tell her third husband, **BEN THOMAS**, 31, to take a ride after he argued with her and broke a window on New Year's Day 1998. But by September, the tempestuous couple had reconciled.

Stars: The Next Generation

Jodie goes it alone, Uma meets Maya, and other tales from the celebrity baby boom

ROBERT DE NIRO, 54, and his wife, **GRACE HIGHTOWER**, 44, welcomed a son they called Elliot. De Niro also has four children from previous relationships.

Mum's the word when it comes to identifying the father, but **JODIE FOSTER**, 35, had no problem telling the world that her son (7 lbs. 8 ozs.) would be named Charles. "The baby is just like her. It's going to be hiking in the mountains," says friend Randy Stone.

Actress **KELLI WILLIAMS**, 28, was pregnant throughout the entire second year of ABC's *The Practice*. Son Kiran Ram Sahgal came along eight days after the season wrapped. Dad is writer **AJAY SAHGAL**, 33.

In May, advertising exec **MICHAEL STERN**, 40, and wife **LISA KUDROW**, 35, made a new little friend: Julian Murray. "I'm relieved," said *Friends* costar Matthew Perry. "I thought Lisa was just getting fat."

Flowers and chocolates won't be the only reason supermodel **ELLE MACPHERSON**, 33, remembers Valentine's Day. That's when she gave birth to son Arpad Busson, who is named after his 35-year-old father, a French financier.

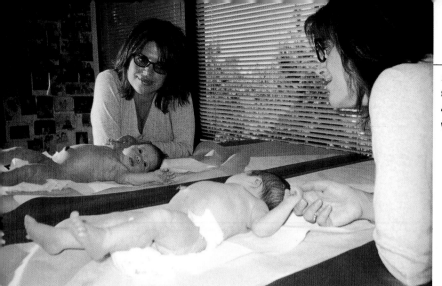

Melrose Place's **LISA RINNA**, 35, says husband **HARRY HAMLIN**, 46, "has fallen in love with another woman"—their daughter Delilah Belle.

ETHAN HAWKE, 27, and wife **UMA THURMAN,** 28, costarred in the film *Gattaca.* They named their next production Maya Ray. The girl (7 lbs. 11 ozs.) was born in New York City.

When Monaco's **PRINCESS STEPHANIE**, 33, gave birth to Camille Marie Kelly Grimaldi, she neither identified the father nor discussed her apparent naming of the girl for the former Grace Kelly, her grandmother.

It is not known if little Jaden Smith, the newborn son of **WILL SMITH,** 30, and **JADA PINKETT SMITH,** 27, is cool enough to "get jiggy wit it," as his father sings. But he springs from a promising gene pool.

Former *MacGyver* hero **RICHARD DEAN ANDERSON,** 48, and his girfriend, **APRYL PROSE**, 32, had their first child, daughter Wylie Quinn, in Vancouver. "I could just sit here staring at her all day," says the proud pop.

"Having a baby and a family is the most important thing one can do," says *Northern Exposure* actress **JANINE TURNER**, 35, seen here with daughter Juliette. Turner won't name the father.

Daughter Emerson Rose (held by daddy **JON TENNEY,** 36) "has totally changed her life," says hairstylist Laurent Dufourg of *Lois & Clark* actress **TERI HATCHER**, 33.

"We'd rather have had a normal upbringing," says Yvonne (right, with Annette and Cecile today, and, below, with all the quints in 1940).

Overdue Justice in Canada

Once displayed like sideshow oddities, the surviving Dionne quints finally get reparations

Six decades ago, in what now seems a stunningly cruel and exploitative act, Cecile Dionne and her sisters—Annette, Yvonne, Emilie and Marie—the world's first-known surviving quintuplets, were taken from their impoverished parents by the Ontario government and displayed in a specially built theme park, called Quintland, to be gawked at by tourists. "Everything was scheduled from 6 in the morning to 6 in the evening," remembers Cecile, 63. "It was like a circus." And a lucrative one at that. Companies paid a trust fund a total of $200,000 a year for the use of their image in ads. And, according to a recent audit, Ontario netted $350 million in quint-generated revenue. Yet by the time the five came of age, most of their share of the trust, once estimated to be worth $15 million, had been spent on the upkeep of Quintland. Far from retiring in luxury, the three surviving quints, all divorced, have been scraping by, sharing Annette's heavily mortgaged Montreal home and Yvonne's $600-a-month librarian's pension. But, belatedly, things are looking up. In March the Ontario government offered the sisters an apology and $2.8 million in compensation. More important, say the women, is the promise of an inquiry into the finances of Quintland—and their stolen youth. (Home, by the way, was hardly better. Returned to their parents at 9, the quints claim they were beaten by their mother and sexually abused by their father.) Only when the investigation ends, says Cecile, "will we rejoice."

56 Across: 'Marry Me?'

Bill Gottlieb is betrothed to Emily Mindel in a crossword puzzle

Manhattan attorney Bill Gottlieb, 27, wanted to propose to Emily Mindel, 24, a law student, ingeniously. "Emily does the puzzle every day," he said, referring to *The New York Times* crossword. "I thought that would be a romantic way." So Gottlieb called *Times* puzzle editor Will Shortz and asked him to play Cupid. When the puzzle ran on January 7, Gottlieb invited Mindel to brunch, then feigned interest in the rest of the paper while Mindel penciled in answers: 38 Across asked for a Gary Lewis and the Playboys hit (THIS DIAMOND RING); 56 Across was a Paula Abdul song (WILL YOU MARRY ME). Other answers included EMILY and BILLG. With only four squares undone, Mindel began to stammer, "This puzzle. . . ." and then gave her reply: an eight-letter phrase for absolutely—"Of course!"

Novel Labor Union

In an unplanned turn of events, three Utah sisters defy all the odds by giving birth on the same day

On March 11, Ernie Carey told his computer science class at Utah Valley State College that two of his daughters had given birth in the last several hours. "What's the probability," asked the proud grandfather, "of my third daughter giving birth on the same day?" With that, his cell phone rang. "Number three is in labor!" he exulted. "Class dismissed!" Despite nearly impossible odds, the sisters—(from left) Karralee Morgan, 28, Marrianne Asay, 27, and Jennifer Hone, 24, all of Orem, Utah—all gave birth on the same day. Though Karralee was due last, she went into labor first. Before going to the hospital, she called her sisters to tell them, "My water broke— don't hate me." Hours after Karralee gave birth, Marrianne went into labor—much to her chagrin. "I didn't want to interfere with Karralee's big moment," she says. Exhausted by the excitement, Jennifer left her sisters at the hospital and went home to nap— until she awoke to contractions. About five hours later, the triple play was completed.

The Royal Show Goes On

Though still reeling from Diana's death, her men have a better year

A Museum at the Spencers' Estate Commemorates Diana

When $15 advance tickets went on sale in January for a still-to-be-finished memorial devoted to the life of Diana, it was obvious that the world's obsession with the late Princess of Wales had not abated. At one point, 10,000 calls were logged in a single minute. By the July 1 opening of the museum's first two-month season, a 12,000-square-foot stable on the Spencer estate at Althorp, northwest of London, had been transformed into a shrine. The exhibits include grainy home movies of a young Di, a photo celebration of her life as Mummy and a gallery of her fabled wardrobe, including her wedding gown.

The Duchess of York Loses Her Mother

In yet another September, Sarah Ferguson, 38, was awakened with a wrenchingly painful and familiar predawn phone call. This time she was at the home of her constant companion, Count Gaddo della Gherardesca, 49, and the news was that her mother (and best friend), Susan Barrantes, 61, had just been killed in a head-on car crash near her ranch in Argentina.

The Highgrove celebration of Charles's 50th birthday brought Camilla Parker Bowles (far left, with sister Annabel Elliot) in formal do. William (bottom) had to change after being whisked in from cadet corps practice at Eton. Charles greeted well-wishers in the city of Sheffield (center).

An Eton Man...Um, Boy

Never much for scholarship, Prince Harry had been struggling with his studies since his mother's death. So the choice of a secondary school, after six years at Ludgrove, was a matter of some concern. Ultimately dad Charles settled on Eton, the same place attended by Harry's older brother William. When Harry, 14, looking excited and self-possessed, signed Eton's famous entrance book in September, he was accompanied solely by Charles, William having thoughtfully stayed away in order not to upstage little bro on his big day.

The Heir Becomes Far More Apparent

In a turnaround year, Prince Charles was buoyed by an opinion poll finding that 63 percent of Britons think he'd make a good king. Equally gratifying was the grace with which his two sons handled their first encounter with his paramour, beginning a palship that soon included Camilla's children, 19 and 23. Prince William, 16, offered a witty birthday toast, urging Dad to "give us the full monty." Everyone was cozy except for the Queen and Camilla, who was excluded from the separate Buck House bash for Charles's 50th.

FRANK SINATRA

Conquerer of the mike, the screen and women's hearts, Ol' Blue Eyes
left a legacy of tough-guy glamor as great as his vocal genius

For more than half a century, the seats were sold out. Francis Albert Sinatra was simply the greatest male vocalist in the history of popular music. With his liquid baritone he helped listeners rediscover powers of enchantment in the oldest meaning of that word: a spell that is sung. Yet the fact that he produced one of the defining sounds of the century accounts for only half his legacy. Sinatra was just as well-known as the hard-living, snap-brimmed Chairman of the Board, a tough guy whose way—with songs, with women, with life—was unapologetically his own throughout his tumultuous 82 years.

Sinatra had long been in declining health, reportedly battling bladder cancer and other illnesses. But when he finally died of a heart attack, the world at large, friends and family—his fourth wife, Barbara, and his children Nancy, Frank Jr. and Tina—were somehow not prepared. "He conquered every medium—television, recording, films," says Tony Bennett. "He was just born for what he did." Friend to Presidents, hero to Italian-Americans, Oscar-winning actor and pop culture's first hysteria-inducing teen idol, Sinatra cut a wide swath across the 20th century. "Sometimes I wonder whether anybody ever had it like I had it," he once said of the generation-spanning adoration of his faithful. "It was the damnedest thing, wasn't it?"

It was. From the moment of his birth in Hoboken, New Jersey, Sinatra got some rough handling. The doctor who delivered him used forceps that punctured his eardrum. His mother, Natalie, an Italian-born midwife, was the chief influence in Frank's early life (his father, Martin, was an illiterate former prizefighter and fireman). Sinatra was expelled from high school at 15 for rowdiness and by the following year was singing occasionally at local dances.

The cynosure of all cameras, he was caught at Hoboken City Hall in 1947 and, seven years later (left), recording in L.A.

His first career break came as part of a vocal quartet, the Hoboken Four, which scored a hit on a 1935 radio broadcast. That led to a cross-country tour with other variety acts.

At first, Sinatra stayed close to home, marrying local sweetheart Nancy Barbato and doing radio work from a Jersey nightclub. He came to the attention of bandleader Harry James, who gave him a two-year contract at $75 a week. Within six months, Sinatra had jumped to the even bigger band of Tommy Dorsey and had his first smash single, "I'll Never Smile Again." At 25, the crooner was named top band vocalist by *Billboard.* But his obsession with becoming bigger than Bing Crosby led him to go solo, and an early engagement in New York City caused a riot when 30,000 girls who'd been unable to get in rampaged through Times Square.

Oceans Eleven costars Sinatra, Martin, Davis (seated), Lawford and Bishop bonded in '60.

Joyous when he wed Ava Gardner in 1951, he slit his wrists after they split in 1953.

Exempt from the draft because of his punctured eardrum, Sinatra racked up successes during the war years but chose not to perform for the troops as other noncombatant stars were careful to do during World War II. In the years immediately after, Sinatra made three movies back-to-back, including *On the Town,* one of his best. In 1944 he signed a $1.5 million contract with MGM and moved to Hollywood. That same year, Sinatra, whose extramarital affairs had included such movie stars as Lana Turner and Marlene Dietrich, embarked on a highly public romance with Ava Gardner. "She was the love of his life," says actress Esther Williams, and just as their affair became serious, Sinatra's career began a hard, quick decline. His only two 1948 films bombed. He walked out on Nancy the following year—after she had refused to grant him a divorce—and got caught up in a Senate probe of organized crime. After a fight with Gardner, Sinatra attempted suicide with an overdose of sleeping pills. A few days later he was granted a divorce by Nancy and in 1951 was free to enter into a brief, bumpy marriage with Gardner. At the very lowest point of his career, when Columbia Records canceled his contract, Gardner intervened to get him the break that restored him: the role of Maggio in *From Here to Eternity.* Sinatra won a Best Supporting Actor Oscar and became a star again.

But he lost Gardner. Following a formal separation, Sinatra again tried suicide. At this time his singing voice took on a melancholy depth. With a new record label, Capitol, along with a new arranger, Nelson Riddle, he made some of his greatest albums, including *In the Wee Small Hours, Only the Lonely* and *Songs for Swingin' Lovers.* In the mid-'50s, Sinatra's film career peaked. It was the start of his ring-a-ding-ding days with his Rat Pack pals Dean Martin, Sammy Davis Jr., Peter Lawford and Joey Bishop. In Las Vegas, which became his second base of operation, his interest in the Sands Hotel would help make Sinatra's fortune. In 1966, at age 50, when he was again topping the charts, he married Mia Farrow, 19. But Farrow quickly grew to hate Sinatra's carousing buddies, and they split less than two years later.

As Sinatra grew older, he mellowed, a process accelerated by his marriage in 1976 to Barbara Marx, a former showgirl and the ex-wife of Marx brother Zeppo. The singer also found himself in the good graces of Ronald and Nancy Reagan. He raised money for the Reagan campaign (as he had once done for John F. Kennedy, another of his presidential pals) and organized both Inaugural galas. In turn, Reagan presented Sinatra with the Presidential Medal of Freedom, the nation's highest civilian honor. Almost to the end, Sinatra performed, playing to SRO concert halls. "The audience is like a broad," he once said. "If you're indifferent, endsville." Sinatra, to his credit, never was.

When it reopened in 1986, Manhattan's Carnegie Hall booked the pop maestro.

HARRY CARAY

Rowdy and raucous, the voice of baseball was its No. 1 fan

Since World War II, Harry Caray had been part of the music of the Midwest, a one-man oompah band for baseball. Thanks to Chicago superstation WGN's 50-state reach, Caray gained national fame for his cries of "Holy cow" and his off-key singing of "Take Me Out to the Ball Game"—shirtless at times—over the Cubs' PA system. When he died at 83 of cardiac arrest, Mark Grace, the Cubs' first baseman, said tearily, "I'll miss his silly, crazy butt." Slugger Sammy Sosa followed his home runs with a kiss and salute intended both for his mother and Caray.

A notorious partyer, Caray was a fixture in Second City nightclubs. But if he sometimes resembled a Shriner from hell, Caray was also an astute, acerbically critical play-by-play man, voted to baseball's Hall of Fame in 1989. "I learned a lot from him," says Jack Buck, who called St. Louis Cardinals' games with Caray from 1954 to 1969. "I learned to be honest." Orphaned at 10, Caray, who grew up in St. Louis, was selling basketball backboards in 1943 when he wangled an audition with radio station KMOX. By 1945 he was calling Cards games, and he remained a fixture for 24 seasons. Caray moved to Chicago in 1971, first with the White Sox, later with the Cubs. Though a 1987 stroke slurred his speech, it didn't slow him down. Thrice-married, Caray leaves behind 10 children and stepchildren, 14 grandchildren and a great-granddaughter. He also leaves behind a press box dynasty: Son Skip, 58, is the voice of the Atlanta Braves; and Skip's son Chip, 33, with FOX, had been scheduled to join Granddad in the Cubs' booth. "I'd give anything to be able to do one game with him," said Chip. "Nobody can fill his shoes."

FLORENCE GRIFFITH JOYNER

Called Lightning, the fastest woman on earth ran—and died—that way

When Florence Griffith Joyner suffocated in her sleep after an epileptic seizure at age 38, her fans were stunned. An explosive sprinter, she had set new records—including two that still stand—on her way to three gold medals at the 1988 Seoul Olympics. But the incomparable stylist, who electrified the track world with her low-cut, one-legged spandex bodysuits and her six-inch-long painted fingernails, actually had a history of medical problems.

The seventh of 11 children, she took up running at age 7 in the Watts area of Los Angeles and kept at it even after the diagnosis of a heart murmur when she was in junior high. Her astounding speed led to rumors about performance-enhancing drugs, but she never tested positive for any of them. After suffering a mysterious ailment in 1996 while on an airplane, her doctors told her to "slow down." But the athlete known to millions as FloJo, who had designed sportswear and earned a cosmetology license after retiring in 1989, did not understand those two words. "Everything she did," says business partner Debra Turner, "she did with perfection and class." FloJo and her husband, Al, a 1984 Olympic triple-jump medalist, had parlayed their accomplishments and her lucrative Japanese endorsement deals into a five-bedroom home in Mission Viejo, California, where they lived with their 7-year-old daughter Mary.

HELEN WILLS MOODY

They dubbed her Little Miss Poker Face, but her inner competitive fire dominated tennis for 16 years

In 1923, at age 17, Helen Wills Moody won the U.S. tennis championship, then dominated the courts for the next 15 years. She amassed an astounding 31 Grand Slam titles as well as two golds at the 1924 Paris Olympics, enjoying one 180-match streak during which she never dropped a set. She also racked up eight Wimbledon singles titles, a record until 1990 when a modern rival took her ninth. But, as Moody noted, Martina Navratilova "pumps iron." One of Moody's mixed doubles partners, tennis legend Don Budge, reported that she hit the ball harder than probably any woman but Steffi Graf. To toughen her game, Moody preferred men as practice partners and championed the introduction of shorter, more sensible tennis skirts. She played until she was 82, 10 years before her death of undisclosed causes. While her unexpressive courtside demeanor caused opponent Alice Marble to liken her to Garbo, off-court the California native's charm and brains (she was a Phi Beta Kappa at college) attracted many admirers, including King Gustaf V of Sweden and Charlie Chaplin. Twice-married, Wills was an accomplished artist who once said that tennis and painting were her antidotes for "a restless heart."

ROY ROGERS
He blazed 'Happy Trails' with a smile and a song as ready as his six-shooters

The white-hatted, straight-shooting King of the Cowboys, Roy Rogers represented the best of Hollywood's good guys. Kids cheered him at Saturday matinees—he was America's top cowboy box office attraction from 1943 to 1954—and during his run on TV from late 1951 to 1957. Rogers was a gentlemanly, down-home hero with virtues as solid as the fists he used in screen fights he never started—and never lost. Best of all, he could sing, even while riding his glorious palomino Trigger. In fact, Rogers, who died in his sleep at 86 after two decades of heart problems, was an Ohio farmboy, not a son of the West. But he managed his image shrewdly, pushing more than 400 products bearing his name into sales of $1 billion. In 1968, long after his acting heyday, he helped found the Roy Rogers restaurant chain with the Marriott Corporation. Roy and Dale Evans, his acting and singing partner and wife of 50 years, had nine children between them, including three adopted children and a foster child; three were lost to illness or accident. As a couple they engaged in countless acts of unpublicized kindness, visiting sick children and raising money for them. Rogers often professed ignorance about his appeal, but, says son Dusty of Roy's charm, "He was no different on the screen or off."

GENE AUTRY
This genial, wholesome buckaroo corralled a whole lotta living—and bucks

For generations of Americans weaned on the Singing Cowboy's films, TV series and records, genial, G-rated Gene Autry will forever embody American youth and vitality. "I never considered myself a legend," said Autry, the son of a scrambling Texas livestock trader and his homemaker wife. "I've loved everything I did." That included cutting perennials like "Back in the Saddle Again" and "Rudolph the Red-Nosed Reindeer," as well as buying baseball's Anaheim Angels. "Gene would ride into the sunset," said sidekick Pat Buttram of his friend in the *Forbes* 400. "Now he owns it."

Autry, who died of respiratory failure three days after celebrating his 91st birthday, was just as dapper as ever in his 10-gallon hat and ornately tooled cowboy boots when he made his last trip to Anaheim Stadium in September to see his beloved Angels beat the Kansas City Royals. "We all wanted to win for him," says Angels star-turned-coach Rod Carew. "Everybody loved him." Though he would be disappointed once again by the Angels' failure to make the playoffs, Autry was not about to utter a discouraging word, even at this late date. "I think it's kind of a crime to go back and daydream," he once said when reflecting on his career. "You can't make yourself young again." He spent his last days with his second wife, Jackie, watching pals Jimmy Stewart, Bob Hope and Gary Cooper in films from the Hollywood era that he and two friendly western rivals, Roy Rogers and Tex Allen (who also died in 1998), helped illuminate.

BARRY GOLDWATER

A straight-shooting Mr. Right remade the Republican party

Whether ferrying C-47 cargo planes between India and China as a young airman in World War II or shooting the Colorado River rapids with his grandchildren at 84, Barry Goldwater was never tentative in any endeavor. The specter of defeat that paralyzes so many politicians didn't faze the five-term Republican senator from Arizona. His unvarnished opinions, on everything from civil rights legislation (against) to defoliating Vietnam with nuclear weapons (in favor), earned him both a spectacular thumping at the hands of Lyndon Johnson in the 1964 presidential election and the legacy that he once said he sought: to be remembered as "an honest man who did his best." Through three decades of Washington politics, Goldwater played hard and pitched political bombshells. Once calling Richard Nixon "the most dishonest individual I have ever met," he followed the edicts of his conscience even if they led him to seemingly contradictory positions. In the 1980s he was sometimes shunned by fellow conservatives for standing up to the Christian right over abortion (his first wife, Peggy, who died in 1985, had founded the Arizona chapter of Planned Parenthood) and gay rights (a grandchild is gay). As severe arthritis sapped Goldwater's energy before his death at 89, he became more a monument than a force in the conservative Republican party, though he lived to see the mainstream absorb many of his ideas.

GEORGE WALLACE

The Old South rabble-rouser, shot by a crazed gunman, repented his racist past

For more than a quarter century, George Wallace, a populist exploiter of middle-class grievances, ruled Alabama and profoundly influenced national politics. But his lifelong dream of becoming President was destroyed in 1972 when he was shot by a drifter while campaigning in the Democratic primaries. The bullets left Wallace paralyzed from the waist down, in pain and emotionally broken until his death at 79. "He said that boy had ruined his life," recalls second wife Cornelia (who was divorced from him in 1978). Born on a cotton farm, Wallace won Alabama's Golden Gloves bantamweight title at 15 and, during World War II, flew 10 combat missions in the Pacific. He then battled his way through local offices and a judgeship before reaching the gubernatorial mansion. At the Inaugural for the first of his four terms, he thundered, "Segregation now, segregation tomorrow, segregation forever," and he staged a famous showdown before yielding to a court order allowing integration of the state university in 1963. In retirement he apologized repeatedly, toiling to rehabilitate his image on race.

CARL WILSON

In turbulent times, the youngest brother kept the surfin' Beach Boys afloat

Though he had been diagnosed with lung cancer, Carl Wilson insisted on joining the Beach Boys' 36th anniversary tour last summer. Weakened by chemotherapy, he sometimes had to sit while playing his guitar. Such quiet strength was characteristic of Carl, the junior of the three Wilson brothers, whose songs about California surfer girls, little deuce coupes and teenage angst helped define American rock in the 1960s.

Born in Los Angeles, Carl (in the middle, below) grew up making music with his older brothers Brian and Dennis. Brian was the creative force and main songwriter, Dennis was the drummer, and Carl was the lead guitarist. Occasionally, Carl was also lead vocalist, his voice dominating on such hits as "Good Vibrations" and "God Only Knows." Publicly, the band was led first by Brian, then by cousin Mike Love. But behind the scenes, Carl was often the steadying influence that held the group together. Though the Beach Boys sang of fun and sun, storm clouds were always present. Carl's two brothers had periodic bouts with drugs, and in 1965, Brian suffered a nervous breakdown, which took him off the road. Then in 1983, Dennis drowned in a swimming accident. A father of two sons, Carl was married twice, the second time to Dean Martin's daughter Gina. A heavy smoker until 1987, Carl lived to see the band inducted into the Rock and Roll Hall of Fame in 1988, but he died at 51 when the cancer spread to his brain.

CARL PERKINS

Once a cotton-picker, he went on to pick rockabilly gems on guitar

He backed up Johnny Cash and wrote hits for the Beatles and Dolly Parton, but Carl Perkins never missed their fame or the screaming following of that other young hopeful at Memphis's Sun Records. "I was fighting a battle working with him, knowing I looked like Mr. Ed," Perkins said. Yet, he added, "I never envied Elvis his mansion and all that. All those boys—Elvis, Jerry Lee Lewis, Roy Orbison— they lost their wives, their families. People say, 'All of them went on to superstardom. Where'd you go?' I say, 'I went home. And that's a good place to be.'" Perkins's influence extended far beyond Jackson, Tennessee, where he and his wife of 45 years, Valda, raised four children and where he died at 65 after a series of strokes. A sharecropper's son, Perkins fashioned tunes that melded the rhythms of black work songs with twangy country sounds. They included rockabilly classics like his 1956 anthem "Blue Suede Shoes," the first country, pop and R&B crossover hit.

JUNIOR WELLS

From roots in country blues, he blew into urban soul and funk

Blues singer and harmonica player Junior Wells enjoyed a career that kept growing over five decades. Wells taught himself the harmonica and then, at age 7, played the streets of his native West Memphis, Arkansas, for pocket change. He steeped himself in the blues by listening to harmonica-great Sonny Boy Williamson on the radio, and had a breakthrough in his late teens in Chicago backing up Muddy Waters. In 1958, Wells hit the blues and the college circuits with guitarist Buddy Guy, with whom he recorded a memorable "Hoodoo Man Blues." Before dying of cancer at 63, Wells performed with pop singers such as Van Morrison and Tracy Chapman and filmed *Blues Brothers 2000*.

BENJAMIN SPOCK

The kindly doctor's radical Rx was to turn parenting back to the parents

When Pocket Books approached New York City pediatrician Benjamin Spock in 1941, the publisher had nothing more grandiose in mind than a small parenting manual. But five years later, when the good doctor's guidebook, initially titled *The Common Sense Book of Baby and Child Care,* hit the stores, the 25¢ paperback was an instant smash with its plainspoken message urging parents not to worry too much, to be flexible and, above all, to trust their own instincts. That gentle advice—a radical departure from the stern, rigid practices of traditional child-rearing—proved so appealing that the book eventually sold almost 50 million copies in more than three dozen languages. His book would exert such vast influence that in 1997 LIFE magazine cited Spock as one of "the century's great cultural liberators," along with Freud and the Beatles.

The tweedy, 6'4" Spock, who had two sons and had won a gold medal in crew at the 1924 Olympics, seemed a perfect father figure for young, middle-class families, and he eventually published a series of authoritative volumes. Yet the reassuring doctor (below, in 1974, with quints and their mom) was beset by emotional turmoil at home. His wife, Jane Cheney, who had collaborated on the original book, was hospitalized frequently for paranoid schizophrenia, exacerbated by alcohol. The marriage lasted nearly 50 years, but in 1976, a year after meeting Mary Morgan, a staunch feminist 40 years his junior, Spock divorced to wed her. With Morgan at his bedside, Spock, a longtime left-wing activist who ran for President in 1972, departed life at 94 the way he had urged parents to raise their kids: in loving, protecting arms.

Leo Buscaglia

An apostle of affection, he was a writer who wielded a Midas touch

Known variously as Dr. Love, the Love Merchant and the Hug Doctor, Leo Buscaglia traveled the world dispensing advice and receiving affection. He also parlayed his touchy-feely zest into big bucks. His 15 love books collectively sold more than 10 million copies; his love lectures were socko box office; his love programs built the ratings of public TV. The son of Italian immigrants, Buscaglia began as a speech therapist and became an education professor at the University of Southern California, where a student's suicide prompted him to create a noncredit course called Love 1. Curiously, Buscaglia, who died at 74 of a heart attack, never had a wife or children.

Carlos Castaneda

His lyrical spiritual explorations blurred the divide between fact and fiction

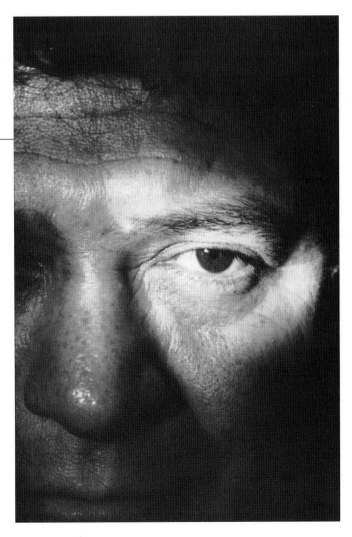

His death was much like his life: mysterious, controversial and riddled with contradictory claims. Though bestselling author Carlos Castaneda died in Los Angeles in April of liver cancer, word of his death did not become public until June. His death certificate was—much like his spiritual writings, detractors would argue—a mix of fact and fiction. Though the document said Castaneda was born in Brazil, he was, in fact, born in Peru; though it said he was never married, he was married once, maybe twice. As for his age, documents variously suggest he was 62, 72 or 74. Whatever the truth, this much is certain: Castaneda's 10 books, tracing the spiritual journey he had taken (or fabricated) as an apprentice to a shaman he called Don Juan Matus, sparked wide interest in New Age spirituality and alternate realities and sold 8 million copies in 17 languages. Scholars dismiss the writings as fanciful science fiction; Castaneda devotees maintain that the Mexican shaman was real. Castaneda, obsessive about his privacy and mostly refusing to be photographed or interviewed, didn't say one way or the other. In his last months, as he was withering from cancer, he taught Tensegrity, a blend of meditation and movement that he said had accounted for his own buoyant health.

ELDRIDGE CLEAVER

Never quite home, he wandered restlessly
across political and geographical borders

Though most remembered as a Black Panther party firebrand in the late '60s and early '70s, Eldridge Cleaver had abandoned the revolution long before his death at 62 from cancer and diabetes. Following a tortuous path that wended through Communism, born-again Christianity, Mormonism and the Unification Church, Cleaver even made stops at clothes designing and the Republican party before finding a measure of peace with a tiny church in Fontana, California, where his girlfriend Tauni Seniff, 50, was board president. He even made the pancakes and hash browns at the church's Easter breakfast. "He loved to cook," says Seniff. "He used to cook in prison."

It was while serving a term in Folsom, California, for assault with intent to kill, that Cleaver, an admitted rapist, penned *Soul on Ice*, the 1968 collection of essays on race that made him a countercultural star. Paroled, he joined the Panthers. Then, following a 1968 gun battle with Oakland police, Cleaver jumped bail and trekked for seven years through Cuba, North Korea and Algeria, taking along his wife, Kathleen (they had two children before their 1985 divorce). Eventually homesickness drew him back for a light sentence—as well as a life that never again seemed to find a center. On Valentine's Day 1997, Cleaver read poetry at a Fontana coffeehouse. His fire seemed gone, and, recalls the manager, "tears welled up in his eyes. He was very apologetic for the things he had done."

BELLA ABZUG

'There are those who say I am impatient, impetuous, uppity'—and one of a kind

She stood out on Capitol Hill by calling for an end to the Vietnam War and the impeachment of Richard Nixon before either position was fashionable. But most Americans remember Bella Abzug as the Woman Who Wore Hats. A feisty, three-term Democratic congresswoman who rarely ventured into public without an eye-popping topper, Abzug was once asked to explain. "When I first became a lawyer [in 1947], only about 2 percent of the bar was women," she said. "People would think I was a secretary. In those days, professional women in the business world wore hats. So I started wearing hats." Not that she needed a gimmick to get attention. During five decades of public life, the raspy-voiced Abzug, who died at 77 after heart surgery, was a fearless advocate for civil rights, women's liberation and her native New York City—for which she once proposed statehood. Her outspoken opinions and bone-cracking handshakes weren't for all. On learning she was attending a 1995 women's rights conference in Beijing, George Bush quipped, "I feel somewhat sorry for the Chinese."

Nonetheless, her achievements were considerable. The daughter of a Russian-immigrant butcher, she studied law at Columbia University and married stockbroker Martin Abzug in 1944. They raised two daughters while Bella worked as a civil rights lawyer in the South and, later, as a peace activist. "In a just country," declared Gloria Steinem, "she would have been President."

Jerome Robbins

He conquered new audiences by taking ballet out of tutus

One of dance's great innovators, choreographer Jerome Robbins combined the lyricism of classical ballet with the razzmatazz of Broadway, leaving behind more than a dozen shows and a repertory of some 60 ballets. From sailors on leave in *On the Town* (1944) to rumbling gang members in *West Side Story* (1957) and an airborne Mary Martin in *Peter Pan* (1954), "he brought ballet to the man on the street," says dancer Stephanie Saland. "His influence not just in dance but also in theater cannot be re-created," says Kevin McKenzie, artistic director of the American Ballet Theater.

"You don't have a boy dancing in a Jewish family," said his Russian émigré dad, but that's what Robbins did until turning to choreography at 34. "He was consumed by his work," says Miami City Ballet director Edward Villella. "Sometimes he would not request but demand." Along the way he lost friends by identifying eight colleagues as members of a Communist arts group before the House Committee on Un-American Activities. Imperious and vigorous until the end, Robbins died at 79 of complications from a stroke. "We were his family," says Saland. "And he was a difficult papa."

Akira Kurosawa

In the world of film directors, he was the grand master

Martin Scorsese, who played Vincent van Gogh in his *Dreams* in 1990, says that the impact of Akira Kurosawa "is so profound as to be almost incomparable." Steven Spielberg calls the Japanese director "the pictorial Shakespeare of our time." A relentless perfectionist who sometimes rehearsed scenes for weeks, Kurosawa left a legacy of 30 films before a stroke ended his career when he was 88. *The Seven Samurai* (1954), his "Far East western" featuring 16th-century Japanese warriors, was an homage to the American movies he adored. Hollywood returned the compliment by remaking it in 1960 as *The Magnificent Seven*. His artistry was rewarded with three Oscars, including one for his influential 1950 classic, *Rashomon*.

LLOYD BRIDGES

Fitness and fatherhood buoyed an actor whose career, at least, never took a dip

In 1989, Lloyd Bridges told the *Chicago Tribune* that he had discovered "the best lesson I could teach my boys," actors Beau and Jeff Bridges: "If you're doing something you really love, you can do it forever." Bridges nearly proved that lesson true. The actor, who died at 85 from natural causes, had rarely slowed during a 57-year career. Jim Abrahams, his director in *Hot Shots! Part Deux* in 1993, recalls a scene in which the actor "leaped off a balcony, hung on to a rope and swung down into a fireplace. That's how he spent his 80th birthday."

His fame began 80 years earlier in San Leandro, California, where he received a baby contest trophy from President Taft. The actor, who gained acclaim as Gary Cooper's deputy in the 1952 film *High Noon,* became a household name as underwater investigator Mike Nelson on the syndicated 1957-61 TV series *Sea Hunt.* The show typecast him as a stone-faced macho man until another generation came to know him as a gruff dimwit in spoofs like *Airplane!* and *Hot Shots!* In his last role, a guest gig on *Seinfeld* as an hilarious geriatric strongman, Bridges looked as fit as he had during his diving days. The other pride of his life was family: Beau, 56, Jeff 48, and Cindy, a homemaker in her mid-40s, with his college-sweetheart wife, Dorothy. "Our most important job," he said in 1986, "is to raise kids to be strong human beings." Certainly his sons' careers gave him satisfaction. "There are times," he noted, "when I look at them, and I feel myself when I was a young blade."

BUFFALO BOB SMITH

'I tried to be the best friend the kids ever had,' he once said, and he seemed to succeed

To millions of rug rats in the 1950s, Buffalo Bob Smith was a surrogate father—the chummy, cheerful host of *The Howdy Doody Show* (1947-60), which costarred a freckle-faced marionette. But to his three sons Ronald, Robin and Christopher, he was the real McCoy: a devoted dad who coached them in Little League and took them to church. Yet even as Smith, 80, lay in the hospital dying of bone cancer, he seemed to be playing to the peanut gallery—the kids in *Howdy*'s live studio audience. "No, slugger, you can't go yet," he told Ronald, now 55. "You've got to give me a kiss—and don't worry, it's not contagious." Certainly, Smith's enthusiasm *was*. Born Robert Schmidt in Buffalo, he was a New York City deejay when NBC tapped him at age 29 to create a kids' TV show. A fixture on the nostalgia circuit since the 1970s, Smith delighted an audience with songs just five months before his death. When he did "It's Howdy Doody Time," 300 misty-eyed baby boomers chimed in.

SHARI LEWIS

Her sock-puppet costars both entertained and enlightened a generation

Two hours after puppeteer Shari Lewis was diagnosed with uterine cancer, she was back working with the fuzzy companions with whom she had delighted kids for four decades. Indeed, the indefatigable Lewis, 65, shot three episodes of her latest PBS series, *The Charlie Horse Music Pizza,* before starting chemotherapy. Two months later she succumbed to pneumonia. The daughter of a college professor and a school music coordinator, Lewis unveiled the sweetly sassy Lamb Chop on *Captain Kangaroo* in 1956. Within four years she had her own program, the first of four that would collect a dozen Emmys. Says her producing partner and daughter, Mallory Tarcher, 36: "I've never known anyone who got more joy out of their career."

LEWIS F. POWELL JR.

He was a peacemaker on a divided Court

It was perhaps no coincidence that after Lewis Powell retired from the Supreme Court in 1987, it took three attempts to fill his seat. (The nominations of Robert Bork and Douglas Ginsburg had failed before Anthony Kennedy was confirmed.) For 15 years, Powell, who died at 90 of pneumonia, had been the High Bench's chief conciliator and builder of consensus. Unfailingly gracious, he was relied upon to restore civility after often-bitter debates about race, abortion and homosexuality. "Underneath that kindness," eulogized Sandra Day O'Connor, "was a firmness and resolve." Apart from World War II service in the Army Air Force, which earned him a Bronze Star, and Harvard Law School, Powell rarely strayed from his native Virginia. He and his late wife of 60 years, Josephine, had four children, nine grandchildren and one great-grandson.

ALAN SHEPARD

He navigated space with a quick wit and icy veneer but a sentimental soul

Swaggering and irreverent, Alan Shepard embodied the brash élan of the early astronauts. He had enthralled the nation in 1961 when, during a 15-minute flight, he became the first American to lift into space. ("They ran out of monkeys," he quipped.) A decade later he charmed us again during the Apollo 14 mission when, with a makeshift six-iron, he smacked a couple of golf balls, in his words, "miles and miles and miles" through the low-gravity lunar atmosphere. "He lived every golfer's dream," Bill Clinton said with a smile in his tribute upon Shepard's death at 74 from leukemia. He was, added the President, "one of the great heroes of modern America."

Known as "the icy commander," Shepard left behind his wife of 53 years, Louise, 76, three daughters, six grandchildren and an extended family from the original Mercury program. "Losing him is like losing a brother," says Gordon Cooper, 71, who, with Shepard and John Glenn, was one of the seven original astronauts. After retiring as a Navy rear admiral in 1974, Shepard made millions in a variety of ventures, including real estate and beer. (As a Coor's distributor, he sometimes made delivery runs himself.) A man whose own space odyssey began in a one-room schoolhouse in rural New Hampshire, he headed the Astronaut Scholarship Foundation, which raised more than $1 million for promising NASA-bound college students. On his Apollo trip, Shepard revealed a softer core, weeping as he beheld Earth from the moon and saying, "It is so lovely, so fragile."

TOM BRADLEY

L.A.'s soft-spoken mayor built coalitions and a new downtown

By the time he was elected Los Angeles's first black mayor in 1973, Tom Bradley had stockpiled 200 pairs of socks—his psychological hedge against poverty. That was because as a kid in Los Angeles, Bradley, the son of a sharecropper and a maid and the grandson of slaves, had been so poor he worked a newspaper route in worn shoes lined with cardboard. Determinedly he joined the LAPD and, while earning a law degree at night school, rose to lieutenant. When that proved the highest rank a black officer could achieve at the time, Bradley moved into politics, first as a member of L.A.'s city council, then as mayor. During five terms he rejuvenated the downtown, remade L.A.'s economy to reflect its diversity and nurtured the city's black middle class. The father of two died at 80 of a heart attack.

FRED FRIENDLY

A formative figure in TV news, he fought to create its golden age

"TV," Fred Friendly once said, "is bigger than any story it reports. It's the greatest teaching tool since the printing press." Friendly, who died at 82 following a series of strokes, was a founding father of broadcast journalism. Born Ferdinand Friendly Wachenheimer, he changed his name when he entered radio in Providence. Then, with his longtime partner Edward R. Murrow, he more or less invented the TV documentary, teaming on the famous 1954 *See It Now* show that demolished the demagogic Sen. Joseph McCarthy. Known for his high standards and unyielding advocacy, Friendly resigned his CBS News presidency in 1966 when the network refused to interrupt regular programming for a Senate hearing on Vietnam. "He never gave up, he never gave in," recalled Dan Rather. Said *60 Minutes* executive producer Don Hewitt (between John F. Kennedy, seated, and Friendly): "I learned more from Fred Friendly than anybody I ever worked with."

RODDY McDOWALL

A familiar screen presence, he was beloved for his discretion and decency

In the final days of his life, Roddy McDowall was, as always, thinking of others. When *Daily Variety,* much to the actor's dismay, reported the day after his 70th birthday that he had terminal cancer, McDowall spent the next week writing and calling pals. "He was calming *me* down," says Carol Burnett. Adds Joanne Carson, Johnny's ex-wife: "[Roddy] was devoted to the art of being a friend." During the course of a 62-year career that spanned film, TV and theater, McDowall was soulmate and trusted confidant to many of Hollywood's biggest stars, from Lauren Bacall and Elizabeth Taylor to Johnny Depp. Yet the discreet McDowall never disclosed any intimacies. "I've had a life crowded by incident and spotted with fascinating individuals," McDowall once said. "I'll just keep the stories to myself."

The son of a merchant seaman and a stage mother, McDowall appeared in the first of his 140 films in Britain, then moved with his family to Hollywood in 1940 to escape the bombing of London. Success quickly followed in such films as *How Green Was My Valley* and *My Friend Flicka*. But soon he found himself typecast. "I was playing 14-year-old parts until I was 23," he once said. In frustration, he relocated to New York City in 1951 to find fresh challenges on Broadway. His famous friendships also led to a successful second career as a celebrity photographer. Summed up Charlton Heston, McDowall's costar in 1968's *Planet of the Apes*: "Roddy was such a nice man, a real decent guy, a gentleman."

JACK LORD

Behind the camera, the 'Book 'em, Danno!' dick was a bit of a dictator

As Steve McGarrett on TV's *Hawaii Five-O,* Jack Lord spent 13 seasons ridding the islands of bad guys. Though he gave up acting soon after the 1980 demise of the show, Lord continued to live in Honolulu, where he died of heart failure at 77. He had appeared on Broadway and in dozens of movies and TV shows, and was also an accomplished artist. Indeed, New York City's Metropolitan Museum of Art acquired two of his prints when he was only 20.

An intensely private man, Lord was known on the series as a temperamental taskmaster who wielded an iron hand over the production. "Jack was a star," says *Five-O* actor Doug Mossman, "and you were aware of it." A fan of poetry, he forced the crew to listen to his readings during lunch. Though he drew praise for casting native Hawaiians, Kam Fong, who played in the series for 10 years, says Lord "never, ever socialized." Lord spent even less time with his own flesh and blood, admitting that he had lost contact in the 1960s with his parents and siblings. While a merchant mariner cruising the Mediterranean in 1942, he married a passenger. Their brief union produced a son whom Lord told a reporter he'd seen only once, and who had died at 13 in an accident. But one relationship did endure: Lord's 26-year marriage to clothing designer Marie de Narde.

E.G. MARSHALL

The initials were Norse (E for Edda, G for Gunnar, a name for kings), but his timber was presidential

If any actor seemed likely to wind up governing the nation, it wasn't the affable Ronald Reagan but, rather, E.G. Marshall, whose granite composure and plainspoken authority would surely have faced down any threat. In a career that spanned six decades, Marshall believably portrayed Presidents (Eisenhower, Truman and Grant, all on TV), senators, tycoons (in 1997's *Absolute Power,* his last movie) and lawyers. Recalls Jack Klugman, one of his costars in the classic 1957 jury movie *Twelve Angry Men:* "You actually believed this man never sweat." In fact, Marshall worked furiously. Most famous (and twice Emmy-honored) for his performance as an impassioned attorney on CBS's *The Defenders,* from 1961 to 1965, he also acquitted himself convincingly as an M.D. on TV's *The Bold Ones* and *Chicago Hope.* Of Norwegian stock, the Minnesota native grew to enjoy hobnobbing with the sort of Washingtonians he so often portrayed. Otherwise, the father of five shunned the spotlight, living quietly with his second wife, Judith. An energetic nature lover to the end, he kept on hiking despite his advancing lung cancer and contracted Lyme disease the year before he died, at 84.

FLIP WILSON

He strutted to prime-time fame on high heels and flamboyant genius

By his own admission, Flip Wilson owed a considerable chunk of his fame and fortune to Geraldine Jones, his distaff alter ego. The character, a wisecracking ghetto queen, introduced such phrases as "the devil made me do it" and "what you see is what you get" into popular discourse in the early '70s. "Geraldine," the comedian once said, "carried me longer than my mother did." But while he will forever be identified with that brassy, bewigged bundle of sass, Wilson, who died of liver cancer at 64 in his Malibu home, had a bag of comic tricks deep enough to keep the nation laughing for years. As the star of NBC's *The Flip Wilson Show* (1970-74), Wilson was TV's first successful black variety show host, earning more than a million dollars a year. His groundbreaking sketches won him two writing Emmys. "His monologues were his," says series producer Bob Henry. "He wrote them—Geraldine, Reverend Leroy [of the Church of What's Happening Now], the invisible dog on a leash. All his."

Born Clerow Wilson, one of 13 children of a Jersey City handyman, Wilson knew from age 5 that he had to be a comedian. Other parts of his life were less predictable. After his mother ran off when he was 7, Wilson spent several years in and out of foster homes. He had two failed marriages and a rumored drug habit, and was estranged from two of his four children. His two sustaining passions remained constant: riding motorcycles and piloting hot-air and helium balloons.

ESTHER ROLLE

A role model both onscreen and off, she refused to buy into Hollywood's clichés

Whether portraying a steel-willed maid or a calm, soothing presence, Esther Rolle never trafficked in facile stereotypes, even as one of TV's most memorable maids, Florida Evans, on *Maude*. Her radar for racial nuance made Florida so popular that CBS spun off a series with Rolle at the center. But two years after *Good Times* premiered in 1974, she balked at the series' buffoonish J.J. character and briefly quit. The 10th of 18 children, Rolle attended Spelman College in Atlanta before breaking into show business as a dancer. A founding member of theater's Negro Ensemble Company, she made several major films, including *To Kill a Mockingbird* (1963) and *Driving Miss Daisy* (1989). Rolle, who suffered from diabetes and died at 78, was the first woman to receive the NAACP's Civil Rights Leadership Award.

MAUREEN O'SULLIVAN

She was a memorable Jane of the jungle queen and Austen varieties

In her 60-year career, Maureen O'Sullivan appeared in more than 60 films, including *Pride and Prejudice* and six as Jane to Johnny Weissmuller's Tarzan (clutching her here in 1936). Later she became almost as well-known as Mia Farrow's mother, a role she played with relish in 1986 in Woody Allen's *Hannah and Her Sisters*. During Farrow's custody battle with Allen, the feisty grandma denounced him as "a desperate and evil man." The daughter of a British Army major, she came to Hollywood from Ireland at 18. "I didn't pretend to be an actress," O'Sullivan admitted. "I just tried to be natural." Married 27 years to director John Farrow, who died in 1963, and 15 to businessman James Cushing, O'Sullivan had seven kids, always putting family first before her death of natural causes at 87.

OCTAVIO PAZ

With his beloved poems and controversial politics, he brought distinction to Mexico

With more than 40 volumes of writing to his credit, all done with a pen, Octavio Paz was Mexico's preeminent poet-essayist until his death of undisclosed causes at 84. A handsome man who as often infuriated the literary left with his conservative politics as he enchanted them with his mesmerizing poems, Paz clashed routinely with other prominent Latino writers. Even so, compatriot Carlos Fuentes conceded that he had "changed forever the face of Mexican literature," and in 1990, Paz received the Nobel Prize. The son of a lawyer, he was seduced from a young age by his novelist grandfather's library, which he described as "an enchanted cave." After dropping out of college, Paz worked variously at magazines, the National Archives and a bank before settling into a 23-year career in the diplomatic service, which posted him to the U.S., France, Japan and India.

ALFRED KAZIN

A literary luminary, he was true to a 'quaint, old-fashioned socialism'

While still an undergraduate at City College in New York City, Alfred Kazin was riding the subway to school one day when a book review he was reading in *The New York Times* so enraged him that he got off the train at Times Square and marched into the *Times* office to complain. The reviewer was so impressed by young Kazin's arguments that he wrote a note to *The New Republic* recommending Kazin as "an intelligent radical" worth hiring. Thus began Kazin's prolific and formidable literary career, involving a mix of memoir, essay and criticism, which spanned 60 years and continued right up until just weeks before his death from cancer at age 83. Four times married, Kazin left two children and a reputation, said Philip Roth, as "America's best reader of American literature in this century." The son of Jewish immigrants from Russia, Kazin grew up in working-class Brooklyn, territory he would later depict evocatively. An unwavering liberal, he crossed swords with old friends, like Irving Kristol and Norman Podhoretz, when their own politics swerved rightward.

"When I was younger," said Kane (in his 70s, in L.A.), "I looked just like Bruce Wayne."

BOB KANE

With a rich imagination, he left the world a gothic legacy called Batman

On a visit to the Warner Bros. lot a few years ago during production of one of their four *Batman* movies, Bob Kane scowled when he passed a wall decorated with studio cartoon stars. "He said, 'Always Bugs Bunny! Where's Batman?'" recalls Paul Levitz, publisher of DC Comics. "So I grabbed some Magic Markers and told him to go at it. He did, and I think Batman and Robin are still on the wall." Kane first drew the moody crime fighter in 1939, and over the next six decades, his caped crusader generated billions from toys, the campy '60s TV show and the *Batman* films.

Though the Brooklyn-born Kane claimed he was "a brooder like Batman," he led a seren-

dipitous life compared to his tragedy-clouded creation. After attending art school in Manhattan, he landed a $25-a-week job with DC Comics in 1938. The next year, assigned to create a hero as successful as Superman, he decided to morph Zorro plus the title character in the movie *The Bat* and a Leonardo da Vinci sketch of a vehicle with batlike wings into his soon-to-be-famous dark dude. "I wanted to create a costume so awesome," said Kane, "that the crooks would be petrified." Stan Lee, 75, a pal and the originator of Spiderman, says he and Kane used to sock each other on the arm while arguing whose superhero was  supreme: "He'd shout, 'Batman!' I'd shout, 'Spiderman!' And we'd go on like that until we broke up laughing. I'm going to miss that laugh." So will Kane's second wife, actress Elizabeth Sanders, 48, in whose arms he died at 83 after an apparent heart attack in their West Hollywood penthouse.

ROB PILATUS

After Milli Vanilli plummeted from fame to infamy, he drowned his disgrace and OD'd

For Rob Pilatus, being half of the German pop duo Milli Vanilli was a labor of dread. After it was revealed in 1990 that he and his Milli mate Fabrice Morvan had sung nary a note on their 1989 album *Girl You Know It's True,* their Grammy for best new artist was revoked and the duo became, in Morvan's words, "the joke of the entire planet." For Pilatus (kneeling), it led to substance abuse, busts and attempted suicide. Despite 10 tries at rehab, he died at 33 from an overdose of drugs and alcohol. "Milli Vanilli was not a disgrace," said Morvan. "The only disgrace is how Rob died—all alone, destroyed from the rapid rise, then sudden fall."

WENDY O. WILLIAMS

The queen of shock rock ended with a jolting finale

Before Madonna and Courtney Love flaunted their blonde ambition, there was Wendy O. Williams, the lead singer of the '80s punk band the Plasmatics. Known for such wild onstage antics as shredding cars with chain saws, she earned a 1985 Grammy nomination before quitting in 1988. But beneath Williams's Mohawk and taped-over nipples lurked a tamer soul. "She was sweet and shy," says her boyfriend and manager Rod Swenson. "Very vulnerable and so sensitive." Too sensitive, it seems. Williams, 48, died of a self-inflicted gunshot wound to the head. She left behind a note that read, in part, "For me, much of the world makes no sense."

Eddie Rabbitt set the pace as a "crossover" artist by topping both the country and pop charts during a recording career that traversed three decades. But the crossover that meant most to Rabbitt, 56, came many years ago, after the Nashville singer-songwriter returned from a six-week road gig to discover that his kids "were about an inch taller" than when he'd left. Thereafter, he told reporters, he was determined to change his ways. "I go out for three or four days," said Rabbitt, "and I'm back for a week, so my kids never really feel that Dad's gone for any deep time." Devoted to Janine, his wife of 21 years, daughter Demelza, 16, and son Tommy, 11, Rabbitt once said that he'd "sort of backed out of the business" in 1985 after his son Timmy died of liver disease before his second birthday. "[Eddie] was a really compassionate, sympathetic person," says longtime friend and fiddle player Bill Rehig. "He was just a sweetheart of a guy."

The son of Irish immigrant parents, Rabbitt (the family's real name) made the improbable journey from a boyhood in Brooklyn to a career in country after moving to Nashville in 1968. Despite scoring 17 No. 1 country tunes, as well as the 1980 pop hits "I Love a Rainy Night" and "Drivin' My Life Away," Rabbitt was proudest of his success as a family man and in charitable work. After Timmy died, Rabbitt said, "it was a time to be with people I love." Nevertheless, he continued to record until 1997, the start of his yearlong battle with lung cancer.

EDDIE RABBITT

He ruled both the pop and country charts but felt like a king only when off the road

BETTY CARTER

An innovative scat cat, she composed and
retooled the jazz canon to make it her own

Her motto was, "It's not about the melody," and every time Betty
Carter tore into a song, it was easy to understand why. Renowned
for her scatting skills, the legendary jazz vocalist reworked standards and rendered her own compositions. Dubbed Betty Bebop by
Lionel Hampton, who had hired Carter to sing with his band and
write some of the arrangements, she also shared the stage with
Miles Davis, Sonny Rollins and Ray Charles, with whom she
recorded an album in 1961 that featured their enduring version of
"Baby, It's Cold Outside." The Michigan native won many honors,
including a Grammy in 1988 and the National Medal of Arts in
1997. Carter, who died of pancreatic cancer at 68, was also known
for her nurturing of young jazz talent. "I'm going to die eventually,"
she once said, "and I don't want it to die with me."

TAMMY WYNETTE

An outsize superstar,
she sang from the very
depths of an unhappy heart

In 1974, Wynette Bird enrolled at
the American Beauty College in
Birmingham, Alabama. Just 22 and,
worse—three months pregnant, trying to raise two young daughters
and recently separated from her husband—Bird had the fantastic notion
of someday becoming a country
singer. The other beauticians thought
she wouldn't last much longer than a
perm. "She was lousy then," recalls
classmate Nancy Frascatore. "I
never in a million years thought that
girl would amount to anything."

Talk about bum predictions: As
Tammy Wynette, Bird fulfilled her
most outlandish dreams. With teary
anthems, including "Stand By Your
Man" and "D-I-V-O-R-C-E,"
Wynette became a hardscrabble-to-
sequins sensation, reigning as First
Lady of Country and selling 30 million records. Wynette was equally
renowned for battling decades of
physical and emotional crises. The
most tormented was her 1969 marriage to her girlhood idol, honky-
tonk heartbreaker George Jones, and
for six clamorous years they were
Nashville's answer to Liz and Dick.
A total of four marriages failed
before she settled into a happy, 20-
year finale with her manager George
Richey. Wynette, a mother of six, also
suffered periods of depression and an
addiction to painkillers, born of
chronic medical ailments that resulted
in some 17 major surgeries. She was
just 55 when she developed the blood
clot in her lungs that killed her.

HENNY YOUNGMAN

As the King of One-Liners, he kept us in stitches

There wasn't a dry eye in the chapel as the 500 mourners heaved —with laughter—while Alan King read Henny Youngman's will: "To his nephew Irving, who asked to be mentioned in his will— 'Hello, Irving!'" Called the world's hardest-working comedian, Youngman was still doing two shows a night just two months before his death of pneumonia at 91. He listed his Manhattan home number in the phone book so he wouldn't miss any jobs, and until the end he continued to try out lines on waiters and construction workers he encountered on the street. Onstage he would fire up to eight jokes a minute, even at bar mitzvahs. Born in 1906 in London ("I was so ugly, the doctor slapped my mother"), Youngman and his Russian immigrant parents moved to Brooklyn, where he grew up near his pal Jackie Gleason. As a child he took up the violin and eventually led a band. He got on the laugh track when he replaced a no-show comedy act at a 1920s gig. His late wife of 58 years, Sadie, weathered his zingers ("Take my wife— please!") good-naturedly. At the memorial service, Jerry Stiller mused, "Is it possible that God himself needed a laugh?"

ROBERT YOUNG

The reassuring smile of America's favorite dad masked a deep insecurity

The tributes that followed Robert Young's death, at 91 from respiratory failure, made a fitting coda to a life well-lived. "He was the father I never had," says Lauren Chapin, who played his younger daughter on *Father Knows Best.* With his real-life family (right, in the '50s), affirms Betty Lou Gleason, one of four daughters Young had with Betty, his wife and soulmate of 61 years, "he was very much like he was on TV. He was a great friend, a wonderful dad."

In a career spanning six decades, Young put his all-American face everywhere—in about 100 films, in much-satirized Sanka coffee commercials and, of course, as the beloved dad in *Father* and as the wise healer *Marcus Welby, M.D.* Young won two Emmy Awards for *Father,* which ran from 1954 to 1960, and another for *Welby,* which made its debut in 1969 and became the next season's highest-rated show.

But there was a side to Young that didn't fit his wholesome image. Since his early 40s, the Chicago native had battled alcoholism and chronic depression. "I was full of terror and fright," he told PEOPLE in 1987. "I drank to escape reality." Four years later, drinking again, Young tried to kill himself. He had shared only with Betty the depth of his despair, and he missed her when she died in 1994. But otherwise, thanks to treatment and medication, Young's final years, says Gleason, were "quite splendid."

PICTURE CREDITS

FRONT COVER (Oprah Winfrey) Janet Gough/Celebrity Photo; (Leonardo DiCaprio) Alex Lentati/Evening Standard/Solo; (Cameron Diaz) Sante D'Orazio/Visages; (Michael J. Fox) Michael O'Neill; (Mark McGwire) Sporting News/Archive Photos; (Calista Flockhart) ©Isabel Snyder/Outline; (Bill Clinton) J. Scott Applewhite/AP

BACK COVER (Florence Griffith Joyner) Manny Millan; (Katie Couric) ©George Lange/Outline; (Streisand/Brolin) Rose Prouser/Sipa Press; (Frank Sinatra) Ken Veeder/©1978 Capitol Records/MPTV

PEOPLE'S PEOPLE 4 Jeff Slocomb/Outline • 6 George Lange/Outline • 7 Andrew Brusso/Outline • 8 Andrew Southam/CPI • 9 Fergus Greer/Janet Botaish Group • 10 Sante D'Orazio/Visages • 11 Michael O'Neill/Outline • 12 (left to right) Mirek Towski/DMI; Jim Spellman/Ipol; Paul Fenton/Shooting Star • 13 (left to right) Arnaldo Magnani/Gamma Liaison; Pierre Zon Zon/South Beach Photo; Victor Malafronte/Celebrity Photo • 14 Michael O'Neill • 15 Robert Fleischauer/Lamoine

HEADLINERS 16-17 Dirck Halstead/Gamma Liaison • 18 Robert Visser/Sygma • 19 (clockwise from top) CNN; Stephane Ouzeau/ Zuma Press; Steven Georges/Long Beach Press-Telegram/Sygma; Geoffrey Hartmann/Sygma • 20-21 (clockwise from bottom left) Robert Borea/AP; Win McNamee/Reuters/Archive Photos; Associated Press/AP (5); ©Haviv/SABA • 22 Ann States/SABA • 23 (top) courtesy Paula Johnson; Gary Cameron/Reuters/Archive Photos • 24 Joe Marquette/AP • 25 (top to bottom) Everett Collection; John T. Barr/Gamma Liaison; Susan Sterner/AP • 26 (clockwise from top) Mark Humphrey/AP; ABC News/AP; courtesy Wright family; David Howell/Sutcliffe News/Sipa Press • 27 (top to bottom) Ho/AP; Ben Margot/AP; The Register Guard/Paul Carter/Sygma • 28 ©Pacemaker/Sipa Press • 29 (top) Eric Miller/Gamma Liaison; Titan Sports/Sygma • 30 Andrew Medichini/AP • 31 (top) Bill Greene/The Boston Globe; Chitose Suzuki/AP • 32 ©Scott F. Schafer/Outline • 33 (top) Lisa Rose/Globe Photos; Nick Ut/AP • 34 Ben Desoto/Houston Chronicle • 35 Michael O'Neill • 36 Richard Alan Hannon • 37 (top to bottom) XENA/courtesy www.mattshepard.org; Ed Andrieski/AP; Martin Simon/SABA • 38 (top) Robin Bowman; L.M. Otero/AP • 39 David Allocca/ DMI • 40 (top) The Seattle Times/Gamma Liaison/Pool; Gary Matoso • 41 Mike Siegel/The Seattle Times/Gamma Liaison • 42 (top) Associated Press/AP; Ilkka Uimonen/Sygma • 43 (top) Ilkka Uimonen/Sygma; Reuters/Paul Hanna/Archive Photos • 44 (left) UPI/Corbis-Bettmann; Peter Jordan/PA News • 45 ©Mary McCartney

PARTY ANIMALS 46 Reuters/Sam Mircovich/Archive Photos • 47 Sean Hahn • 48 (left to right) Lisa Rose/Globe photos; Sean Hahn; Lisa Rose/Globe Photos • 49 (top to bottom) Ron Davis/Shooting Star (2); Michael Caulfield/AP • 50-51 (clockwise from top left) Fred Prouser/Reuters/Archive Photos; Lisa Rose/Globe Photos; Kathy Hutchins; Nina Prommer/Globe Photos; Lisa Rose/Globe Photos (2) • 52 (top to bottom) RC ATAS/NATAS; Steve Granitz/Retna Ltd.; Fitzroy Barrett/Globe Photos • 53 (clockwise from top right) Jim Ruyman/UPI; Ron Davis/Shooting Star; Nick Falzerano/Mazur; Rose Prouser/Reuters/Archive Photos • 54 (clockwise from top right)© Patrick McMullen; Aaron Montgomery/JPI; Gregory Pace/Sygma • 55 (clockwise from right) Steve Granitz/Retna Ltd.; ©Screen Actors Guild; Steve Granitz/Retna Ltd. (2) • 56 (clockwise from top right) Bill Davila/Retna Ltd.; The Recording Academy; Mitch Gerber/Corbis; Bill Davila/Retna Ltd. • 57 (clockwise from bottom) Tammie Arroyo; Lisa Rose/Globe Photos (2); Jackson Goff • 58 Lisa Rose/Globe Photos (3) • 59 Robin Platzer/Twin Images (3) • 60 (clockwise from top right) Steve Granitz/Retna Ltd.; Kevin Winter/Celebrity Photo; Lisa Rose/Globe Photos • 61 (clockwise from top right) Steve Granitz/Retna Ltd.; Kevin Mazur; VH1 Fashion Awards designed by Miuccia Prada; Jeff Christensen/Gamma Liaison

SENSATIONS 62-63 Mousse/MAXPPP; (inset) Elizabeth Lippman • 64 (top) © Patrick McMullen; Mario Brenna/Jason Fraser • 65 (clockwise from top right) Kimberly Butler; Jeff Christensen/Gamma Liaison; Atsushi Tsukada/AP • 66 (top) Gerry Gropp; Ken Regan/Camera 5 • 67 Stephen Trupp/Star Max • 68 V.J. Lovero/Sports Illustrated • 69 (top) Sporting News/Archive Photos; Reuters/Tim Parker/Archive Photos • 70 (left) Neal Preston/Outline; BIG Pictures USA • 71 (left to right) Dave Hogan/All Action/Retna Ltd.; Kevin Mazur; BIG Pictures USA • 72 Rankin/Dazed and Confused/Camera Press/Retna Ltd. • 73 Kwaku Alston/Outline • 74 Maureen Donaldson • 75 (clockwise from bottom left) Stephen Ellison/Outline; Susan Rothchild/Harper Perennial; Donna Day • 76 Ed Reinke/AP • 77 (top) John Biever/Sports Illustrated; David Klutho/Sports Illustrated • 78 (top) Adam Knott; Andrew Eccles/The WB Television Network • 79 (top to bottom) Todd Eberle/ Sygma; Globe Photos; Photofest • 80 George Lange/Outline • 81 (top) Jim McHugh/Outline; Screen Scenes

SECOND CHANCES 82 Shelly Katz/Gamma Liaison • 83 (top) Paul Howell/Gamma Liaison; Sygma • 84 (clockwise from top right) courtesy Connie and Jim Hickerson; Kimberly Butler; Taro Yamasaki • 85 (top) Carol Ford; Linda Rosier • 86 (clockwise from top right) Ann States/SABA; Lisa Means; Martin Simon/SABA • 87 (top to bottom) Brian Smith/Outline; Claro Cortes IV/Reuters/Archive Photos; Robert Clark

FAMILY MATTERS 88 McNew/Sipa Press • 89 Deborah Wald/Outline • 90-91 (clockwise from left) Arthur Elgort/AP; Walter Dhladhla/PA/Reuters/Archive Photos; Olympia/Sipa Press; Sarah Lyman; London Features; Firooz Sahedi/San Francisco Examiner/Zuma Press • 92-93 (clockwise from top left) BIG Pictures USA; Rex Features; John Roca/NY Daily News; Ethan Miller/Corbis; Alex Berliner/Berliner Studios; Ron Wolfson/London Features; Steve Heaslip/Cape Cod Times/Sipa Press • 94-95 (clockwise from top right) Elayne Lodge; Sonia Moskowitz/Globe Photos; Paul Smith/Retna Ltd.; Agostini/Gamma Liaison; Kevin Mazur • 96-97 (clockwise from top left) Miranda Shen/Celebrity Photo; Sonia Moskowitz/Globe Photos; Tony Costa/Outline; John Paschal/Celebrity Photo; Steve Granitz/Retna Ltd.; B.B. Beans/Ipol; Evan Agostini/Gamma Liaison; Russ Einhorn/Gamma Liaison • 98 (left) Eric Robert/Sygma; Janet Botaish Group • 99 (top to bottom) Vinnie Zuffante/Star File; Ann Summa; Tony Duran • 100 (clockwise from bottom right) Barry King/Shooting Star; David Allocca/DMI; courtesy Lisa Rinna • 101 (top to bottom) Neal Preston/Outline; courtesy Janine Turner; Lexington Herald/Sygma • 102 (top) Taro Yamasaki; Hansel Mieth/Life • 103 (top) Todd France; Acey Harper • 104 (bottom) David Long/Nunn Syndication Ltd. • 105 (top to bottom) Ken Goff; Adrian Sherratt/News International Syndication; Ken Goff; Philip Ide/Rex USA

TRIBUTE 106 Sid Avery/MPTV • 107 Ed Shirak/Our Way/Sygma • 108 (clockwise from top right) Irving Haberman/Three Trees Entertainment/Christie's Images; UPI/Corbis-Bettmann; Sid Avery/MPTV • 109 Hal Stoelzle/Sports Illustrated • 110 Ken Regan/Camera 5 • 111 Archive Photos • 112 Ben Carbonetto Collection • 113 Thomas McAvoy/Life • 114 UPI/Corbis-Bettmann • 115 UPI/Corbis-Bettmann • 116 Michael Ochs Archives • 117 (top) Jim Smeal/Galella Ltd.; Michael Ochs Archives • 118 AP • 119 (top) Tony Korody/Sygma; Eddie Adams/Outline • 120 ©1996 Rene Burri/Magnum • 121 ©1998 Charles Gatewood/Magnum • 122 M. Pelletier/Sygma • 123 Loomis Dean/Life • 124 Photofest • 125 (top) Everett Collection; Steve Schapiro • 126 Robert Trippett/Sipa Press • 127 Archive Photos • 128 (top) Phil McCarten/Los Angeles Daily News/ Sygma; CBS Photo Archive • 129 Mary Ellen Mark • 130 Michael O'Neill/Outline • 131 Kobal Collection • 132 NBC/Globe Photos • 133 (top)CBS Photo Archive; Archive Photos • 134 (top) Susan Meiselas/ Magnum; Inge Morath/Magnum • 135 (top) ©1998 Jonathan Exley; ©DC Comics/NPC • 1136 (top) Craig Fujii/AP; Mary Ellen Mark • 137 ©Peter Nash/Michael Ochs Archives • 138 Andrew Eccles/Outline • 139 David Redfern/Retna Ltd. • 140 Michael Baytoff/Outline • 141 Archive Photos

A

Abdul, Paula 94
Abzug, Bella 121
Academy Awards 46-49
Academy of Country Music
    Awards 60
Adams, Victoria 73
Affleck, Ben 48-49
Afshar, Shiva 53
Albert, Marv 85
Alexander, Jason 80
Alley, Kirstie 58
Amanpour, Christiane 91
American Comedy
    Awards 60
American Music Awards 61
Amos, Tori 93
Anderson, Richard Dean 101
Aniston, Jennifer 95
Anspaugh, David 97
Asay, Marrianne 103
Autry, Gene 112-113

B

Baby Switch case 22-23
Backstreet Boys 72
Baldwin, Alec 47
Barrantes, Susan 104
Barrymore, Drew 48, 79
Basinger, Kim 47
Beach Boys 116
Beckerman, Brad 94
Beckham, David 73
Bergen, Candice 81
Best and Worst Dressed,
    PEOPLE's 1998 12-13
Bingham, Traci 92
Bishop, Joey 108
Blaine, David 64
Bono, Mary 24-25
Bono, Sonny 24-25
Bowles, Camilla Parker 105
Bradley, Tom 128
Bridges, Lloyd 124
Brolin, James 88-89
Bronstein, Phil 90
Brown, Bobby 52
Brown, Melanie 73
Buscaglia, Leo 119
Bye, Karyn 77

C

Cameron, James 49, 95
Campbell, Neve 8
Caray, Harry 109

Carey, Drew 61
Carrey, Jim 60
Carter, Betty 138
Carter, Deana 56
Carter, Nick 72
Castaneda, Carlos 119
Castro, Fidel 43
Charles, Prince of Wales 105
Cher 25
Cleaver, Eldridge 120
Clinton, Bill 16-21, 86
Clinton, Chelsea 20
Clinton, Hillary 20-21
Combs, Sean "Puffy" 12
Country Music Awards 57
Couric, Katie 6
Crawford, Cindy 90
Crystal, Billy 52
Culkin, Macaulay 91
Curtis, Tony 93

D

Damon, Matt 48-49
Davis, Sammy, Jr. 108
Dawson, George 86
DeGeneres, Ellen 37
De Niro, Robert 98
Diana, Princess of Wales
    104-105
Diaz, Cameron 10
DiCaprio, Leonardo 62-65
Dion, Celine 56
Dionne quintuplets 102
Dixie Chicks 57
Donovan, Tate 95
Dorough, Howie 72
Downey, Roma 97
Driver, Minnie 12, 50
Duchovny, David 55
Dunn, Tricia 77

E

Electra, Carmen 13
Elfman, Jenna 58
Elise, Kimberly 66
Emmys, Daytime 54
Emmys, Prime-Time 52-53
Erwin, Emily 57
Evangelista, Linda 96
Evans, Linda 97
Everett, Rupert 51

F

Farmer, James 86
Faulkiner, Heather 85
Fawcett, Farrah 39
Ferguson, Sarah 104
Fielding, Helen 75
Flockhart, Calista 4
Folkman, Judah 31
Fonda, Bridget 96
Fonda, Peter 50-51
Ford, Harrison 2, 14, 58
Foster, Jodie 98
Fox, Michael J. 35
Friendly, Fred 128
Frye, Soleil Moon 93
Fualaau, Vili 40-41

G

Gabrielson, Kristin 84
Gardner, Ava 108
Gerber, Rande 90
Gibson, Thomas 58
Glenn, John 82-83
Goldberg, Jason 93
Goldberg, Whoopi 58
Golden, Andrew 26-27
Golden Globe Awards 50-51
Goldwater, Barry 114-115
Gore, Tipper 42-43
Gottlieb, Bill 103
Grammer, Camille 52-53
Grammer, Kelsey 52-53
Grammy Awards 56
Grillo, Frank 54
Gulzar, Jimmy 73

H

Haas, Lukas 64
Halliwell, Geri 1, 72-73
Hamilton, Linda 95
Hamlin, Harry 100
Harry, Prince 105
Hartman, Brynn 33
Hartman, Phil 32-33
Hatcher, Teri 101
Hawke, Ethan 100
Hawley, Mark 93
Hawn, Goldie 51
Hefner, Hugh 95
Hefner, Kimberly Conrad 95
Henderson, Russell 36-37
Herbst, Rebecca 54
Hermann, Peter 54
Herzigova, Eva 64

Hightower, Grace 98
Hill, Faith 60
Hill, Lauryn 70-71
Hockey Team, U.S.
    Women's 77
Hoffman, Dustin 50
Hone, Jennifer 103
Houston, Whitney 52
Hume, John 28
Hung, Sammo 78
Hunt, Helen 49
Hurricane Mitch 42-43

I

Imbruglia, Natalie 70
Ingram, Bob "Doc" 87

J

Jewel 56
John Paul II, Pope 43
Johnson, Mitchell 26-27
Johnston, Kristen 55
Jones, Paula 19
Joyner, Florence Griffith
    110-111
Judd, Wynonna 97

K

Kane, Bob 135
Kazin, Alfred 134
Kelley, Arch 97
Kennedy, Douglas 92
Kinkel, Kip 26-27
Krakowski, Jane 59
Kudrow, Lisa 99
Kurosawa, Akira 122

L

LaNasa, Katherine 92
Larry Sanders Show, The 81
Lauer, Matt 93
Lawford, Peter 108
Lawrence, Stacie 96
Lawrence, Tracy 96
Leoni, Téa 55
Letourneau, Mary Kay 40-41
Lewinski, Monica 16-17, 19
Lewis, Jerry 60
Lewis, Shari 125
Lipinski, Tara 3, 48, 76-77
Littrell, Brian 72
Lord, Jack 130-131
Louis-Dreyfus, Julia 80

M

Machel, Graça *90*
MacLachlan, Kyle *96*
Macpherson, Elle *99*
Madonna *61*
Maines, Natalie *57*
Malone, Jena *51*
Mandela, Nelson *90*
Manheim, Camryn *53*
Marshall, E.G. *130*
Martin, Alexandra *58*
Martin, Dean *108*
McCarthy, Teresia Benedicta *30-31*
McCartney, Linda *3, 44-45*
McCartney, Paul *3, 44*
McDermott, Dylan *11, 53*
McDowall, Roddy *129*
McGraw, Tim *60*
McGwire, Mark *68-69*
McKinney, Aaron *36-37*
McLean, A. J. *72*
Mindel, Emily *103*
Miner, Rachel *91*
Mitchell, George *28*
Moody, Helen Wills *111*
Moore, Demi *94*
Morgan, Karralee *103*
Morgan, Lorrie *57*
Morgan, Mary *118*
Most Beautiful People, PEOPLE's 1998 *8-11*
Most Intriguing People, PEOPLE's 1998 *4-7*
MTV Movie Awards *60*
MTV Video Music Awards *61*
Murphy Brown *81*

N

Neeson, Liam *59*
Nelson, Chris *84*
Newton, Thandie *66*
Nicholson, Jack *50-51*

O

Oakes, Harry, Jr. *43*
O'Donnell, Rosie *54*
Orr, James *39*
O'Sullivan, Maureen *133*

P

Pak, Se Ri *65*
Paltrow, Gwyneth *12*
Paz, Octavio *134*

People's Choice Awards *58*
Perkins, Carl *117*
Pilatus, Rob *136*
Pitt, Brad *48*
Pollan, Tracy *35*
Powell, Lewis F., Jr. *126*
Prose, Apryl *101*

R

Rabbitt, Eddie *137*
Ragnarsson, Kristjan *38-39*
Randall, Jon *57*
Richards, Michael *53, 80*
Richardson, Kevin *72*
Richardson, Natasha *59*
Rimes, LeAnn *57*
Rinna, Lisa *100*
Robbins, Jerome *122-123*
Roberts, Julia *51*
Rock, Chris *2, 7, 61*
Rogers, Roy *112*
Rolle, Esther *133*
Roque, Annette *93*
Roseanne *97*
Rubin, James *91*
Russell, Keri *78*
Russell, Kurt *51*
Ryker, Jacob *26-27*

S

Sahgal, Ajay *99*
Sanders, Larry *81*
Sandler, Adam *79*
Sang, Lan *38-39*
Screen Actors Guild Awards *55*
Seidel, Martie *57*
Seinfeld *80*
Seinfeld, Jerry *80*
Sexiest Men Alive, PEOPLE's 1998 *14-15*
Shandling, Garry *55, 81*
Sheindlin, Judy *74*
Shepard, Alan *126-127*
Shepard, Dennis *36-37*
Shepard, Judy *36-37*
Shepard, Matthew *36-37*
Sinatra, Frank *106-108*
Smith, Buffalo Bob *125*
Smith, Jada Pinkett *51, 100*
Smith, Will *100*
Sorvino, Mira *96*
Sosa, Sammy *68-69*
Spice Girls *72-73*

Spock, Benjamin *118*
Stark, Molly *92*
Starr, Kenneth *18*
Stein, Edith *30-31*
Stephanie, Princess *100*
Stern, Michael *99*
Stewart, French *92*
Stoltz, Eric *96*
Stone, Sharon *90*
Streisand, Barbra *88-89*
Stringer, Bob *87*

T

Tarantino, Quentin *96*
Taymor, Julie *59*
Tenney, Jon *101*
Teresa Benedicta of the Cross, Sister *30-31*
Thomas, Ben *97*
Thomas, Jim *86*
Thompson, Emma *13*
Thompson, Hugh *87*
Thorne-Smith, Courtney *55*
Thornton, Billy Bob *13*
Threapleton, Jim *91*
Thurman, Uma *100*
Tony Awards *59*
Trimble, David *28*
Tripp, Linda *19*
Tucker, Karla Faye *34*
Turner, Janine *101*

U

Usher *15*

V

Vallier, Robb *92*
Van Der Beek, James *9*
Vanden Berg, Jill *93*
Vanzant, Iyanla *84*
Ventura, Jesse *29*
VH1 Fashion Awards *61*

W

Wallace, George *114*
Watros, Cynthia *54*
Weissmuller, Johnny *133*
Wells, Junior *117*
Wells, Rebecca *75*
William, Prince *105*
Williams, Kelli *99*
Williams, Robin *46-47*

Williams, Wendy O. *136*
Willis, Bruce *94*
Wilson, Carl *116*
Wilson, Flip *132*
Winfrey, Oprah *66-67*
Winkler, Henry *79*
Winslet, Kate *49, 91*
Wright, Shannon *26-27*
Wynette, Tammy *138-139*

Y

Yankovic, Weird Al *61*
Yanni *97*
Young, Robert *140-141*
Youngman, Henny *140*